BUSINESS INTELLIGENCE

AF658298

BUSINESS INTELLIGENCE

Scinthia Clarinda S.
Associate Professor,
Dept of CSE, Sathyabama Institute
of Science and Technology

Sonia Jenifer Rayen
Associate Professor,
Dept of CSE, Sathyabama Institute
of Science and Technology

Lubna Kalam
Associate Professor,
Dept of CSE, Sathyabama Institute
of Science and Technology

KHANNA BOOK PUBLISHING CO. (P) Ltd.
4C/4344, Ansari Road, Darya Ganj,
New Delhi, India

Sathyabama Institute of Science and Technology
Jeppiaar Nagar, Rajiv Gandhi Salai,
Chennai, Tamilnadu, India

Dear Readers,

To prevent the piracy, this book is secured with HIGH SECURITY HOLOGRAM on the front title cover. In case you don't find the hologram on the front cover title, please write us to at contact@khannabooks.com or whatsapp us at +91-99109 09320 and avail special gift voucher for yourself.

Specimen of Hologram on front Cover title:

Moreover, there is a SPECIAL DISCOUNT COUPON for you with EVERY HOLOGRAM.

How to avail this SPECIAL DISCOUNT:

Step 1: Scratch the hologram
Step 2: Under the scratch area, your "coupon code" is available
Step 3: Logon to www.khannabooks.com
Step 4: Use your "coupon code" in the shopping cart and get your copy at a special discount
Step 5: Enjoy your reading!

Thanks,
Khanna Publishing House

ISBN: 978-93-55386-42-7

Business Intelligence
by **Scinthia Clarinda S.;**
Sonia Jenifer Rayen;
Lubna Kalam

First Edition: 2025

To view complete list of books, please scan the QR Code:

Published by:
Khanna Book Publishing Co. (P) Ltd.
CIN: U22110DL1998PTC095547

Visit us at: www.khannabooks.com
Write us at: contact@khannabooks.com

Printed in Bharat.

Copyright © Publisher

No part of this publication may be reproduced, stored in a retrieval system or transmitted, in any form or by any means, electronic, mechanical, photocopying, recording or otherwise without prior permission of the publisher.

This book is sold subject to the condition that it shall not, by way of trade, be lent, re-sold, hired out or otherwise disposed of without the publisher's consent, in any form of binding or cover other than that in which it is published.

Disclaimer: The website links provided by the author in this book are placed for informational, educational & reference purpose only. The Publisher do not endorse these website links or the views of the speaker/ content of the said weblinks. In case of any dispute, all legal matters to be settled under Delhi Jurisdiction only.

Preface

In today's data-driven world, organizations are increasingly relying on Business Intelligence (BI) to transform raw data into actionable insights. This report aims to provide a comprehensive overview of the BI strategies, tools, and methodologies that can empower decision-makers to optimize performance, increase efficiency, and enhance business outcomes. By analyzing data from various sources, BI enables businesses to identify trends, forecast future performance, and make well-informed, data-backed decisions. This document will explore key BI concepts, the implementation of BI systems, and the best practices that organizations can adopt to maximize the value of their data. The focus is on how BI can help streamline operations, improve customer insights, and foster a more agile, responsive enterprise.

This book is structured to guide readers through the entire BI journey, from foundational principles to strategic planning. We begin with Unit 1: Business Intelligence Introduction, establishing the core concepts and value proposition of BI. We then move into the practical application with Unit 2: Business Intelligence Life Cycle, detailing the systematic steps from data acquisition to insight delivery. Understanding who uses BI is critical, which is covered in Unit 3: Business Intelligence User Model, exploring the needs of various stakeholders from executives to analysts. Recognizing that the path to data excellence is not without obstacles, Unit 4: Business Intelligence Issues and Challenges addresses common hurdles like data quality, governance, and technology adoption.

Finally, we conclude with the strategic blueprint in Unit 5: Business Intelligence Strategy and Roadmap, providing a framework for developing and implementing a successful, long-term BI initiative.

Contents

Business Intelligence Introduction

1

UNIT

RATIONALE

Understanding Business Intelligence (BI) fundamentals is crucial for navigating today's data-driven world. This unit introduces core BI concepts, demonstrating how organizations transform raw data into actionable insights. It covers data types, BI lifecycles, and strategic frameworks, highlighting how these elements empower informed decision-making. By grasping these principles, individuals can effectively contribute to leveraging data for business growth and competitive advantage.

1.1 INTRODUCTION

What is Data?

Data, in its simplest form, is a collection of raw facts. It represents something—anything—from numerical values and written words to visual images, audio recordings, or sensor outputs. It's the building block that, when given meaning through organization, analysis, and context, transforms into useful information.

Data can be broadly categorized into two types :

- **Structured Data:** This is data that's neatly organized and formatted, typically fitting into a predefined structure like rows and columns in a database or spreadsheet. Think of it as data that's easy to categorize and search, like customer details, sales records, or transaction timestamps. Its organized nature makes it straightforward to process and analyze.
- **Unstructured Data:** This is data that lacks a fixed format or structure. It's often rich in text, but can also include multimedia content like images, audio, and video. Examples include emails, social media content, documents, and recordings. Unstructured data presents analysis challenges due to its lack of a rigid structure, but advancements in AI and natural language processing are increasingly enabling us to derive valuable insights from it.

1.2 INFORMATION VS INTELLIGENCE

Data vs. Information

- **Data:** Data is the foundation of knowledge, consisting of raw, unrefined facts and figures. Picture it as the collection of unorganized numbers, text, or symbols gathered from various sources.

- **Information:** Information is data that has been processed, structured, and given context. It's data that has been transformed into something meaningful and relevant for decision-making.

Characteristics of Information

- **Accuracy and Timeliness:** It's dependable and available when needed.
- **Specificity and Organization:** It's tailored to a purpose and presented in a structured way.
- **Contextual Relevance:** It's placed within a framework that provides meaning.
- **Actionable Insights:** It leads to greater understanding and reduces uncertainty, enabling informed choices. Essentially, data is the "what is," and information is the "what it signifies."

Figure 1.1: *Structured with Unstructured Data*

Business Intelligence (BI)

BI is a comprehensive set of processes, architectures, and technologies that transform raw data into valuable information. It's about converting data into actionable insights that drive profitable business outcomes. BI systems utilize software and services to analyze data and generate valuable insights.

Why BI is Important?

- **Measurement:** BI enables the creation of Key Performance Indicators (KPIs) based on historical data, allowing organizations to track progress and performance.
- **Benchmarking:** BI systems help identify and establish benchmarks for various business processes, facilitating performance improvement.
- **Market Trend Analysis:** Organizations can identify market trends and spot emerging business problems, enabling proactive decision-making. Data Visualization: BI enhances data quality through visualization, leading to improved decision-making.
- **Accessibility:** BI systems are valuable for both large enterprises and small and medium-sized enterprises (SMEs).

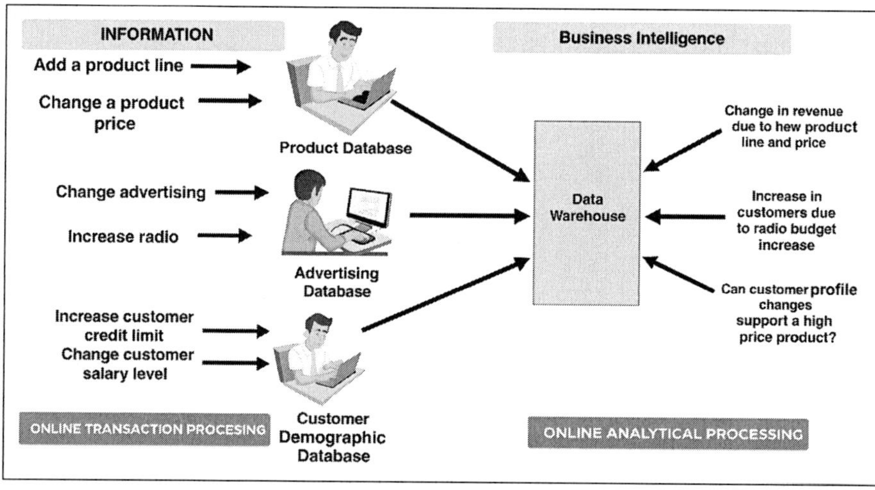

Figure 1.2: *Example of Business Intelligent System*

History of BI

- **Early Stages (1970s):** Management Information Systems (MIS) provided static, two- dimensional reports with limited analytical capabilities.
- **Executive Information Systems (EIS) (Early 1980s):** EIS expanded computerized support to top-level managers, introducing features like: Dynamic multidimensional reporting, forecasting and prediction, trend analysis, and drill-down capabilities.
- **The Rise of BI (Mid-1990s):** The term "Business Intelligence" was coined by Gartner Group. Many of the capabilities of EIS were incorporated into BI systems, along with new functionalities. BI systems became comprehensive enterprise information systems.
- **Modern BI (2005 onwards):** BI systems began integrating artificial intelligence (AI) and advanced analytical capabilities. A greater push towards real-time analytics.

Types of BI Users

- **Professional Data Analyst:** These users delve deeply into data to find trends and build sophisticated business strategies using advanced statistical analysis.
- **IT Users:** IT professionals are responsible for maintaining and managing the BI infrastructure.
- **Company Executives (CEO/CXO):** Executives use BI to improve operational efficiency and drive profitability.
- **Business Users:** BI is used across all areas of a business. There are two general types:
  - **Casual Business Intelligence User:** users that are interested in general reporting, and pre-generated reports.
  - **Power Users:** users that are wanting to find in depth information, build reports, and perform data analysis.

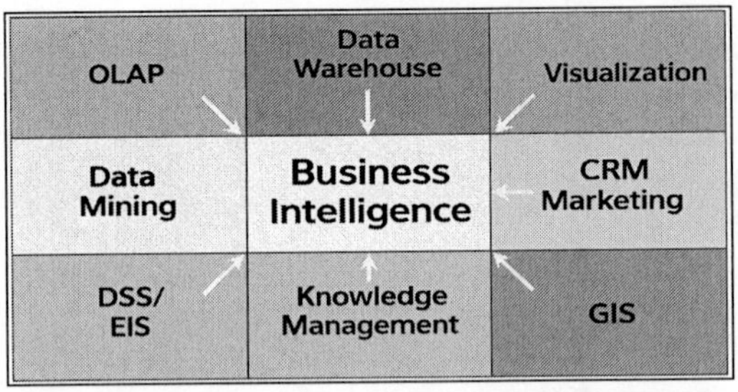

Figure 1.3: *BI Relation to Other Information Systems*

1.3 COMPONENTS OF BUSINESS INTELLIGENCE ARCHITECTURE

BI's Core Purpose

Business Intelligence empowers organizations to transform raw data into actionable knowledge, facilitating informed decision-making through mathematical models and analytical techniques.

Fundamental Building Blocks of a BI System

- **Diverse Data:** Data originates from various internal and external sources.
- **Varied Data Formats:** It encompasses both structured data from operational systems and unstructured data like emails and documents.
- This is the initial point of data related processes.

Data Storage and Organization

These components provide the storage foundation for BI. Centralized Data:

- A core repository integrating data from multiple sources into a consistent format.
- Designed for analytical processing, not transactional operations.
- Serves as the central point for organized data.

Focused Data

- Subsets of the data warehouse, designed for specific departmental needs.
- Provides quick access to relevant data for targeted users.
- Enables targeted analytical work.

Analytical Techniques

These encompass the tools and methods used to extract insights from stored data.

Goal

- To support decision-making with valuable information.
- To apply mathematical and analytical models to data.

Examples

- **Multidimensional Analysis (OLAP):** Enables data exploration from various perspectives.

- **Pattern Discovery (Exploratory Data Analysis):** Uses statistical methods to find data patterns.
- **Trend Analysis (Time Series Analysis):** Analyzes data over time to identify trends.
- **Knowledge Discovery (Data Mining):** Uses algorithms to find hidden relationships in data.
- **Solution Optimization (Optimization Models):** Uses math to find ideal solutions.

Key Functional Areas of Business Intelligence

Strategic Data Analysis (OLAP)

- Enables executives to analyze aggregated data for strategic oversight.
- Provides rapid, interactive analysis of large datasets.

Performance Prediction (CPM/Advanced Analytics)

- Offers statistical and predictive tools to assess product and service performance.
- Aids in forecasting future outcomes and identifying potential risks.

Dynamic Decision-Making (Real-time BI)

- Allows businesses to quickly respond to market changes and customer behavior.
- Provides real-time insights for immediate action.

Centralized Data Management (Data Warehousing)

- A core component for storing and managing large, diverse datasets.
- Provides a unified data repository for analysis.

Data Preparation (Data Sources)

- The initial point for data collection and preparation.
- Uses software to create structured datasets from raw data.
- The data from these sources are then visualized.

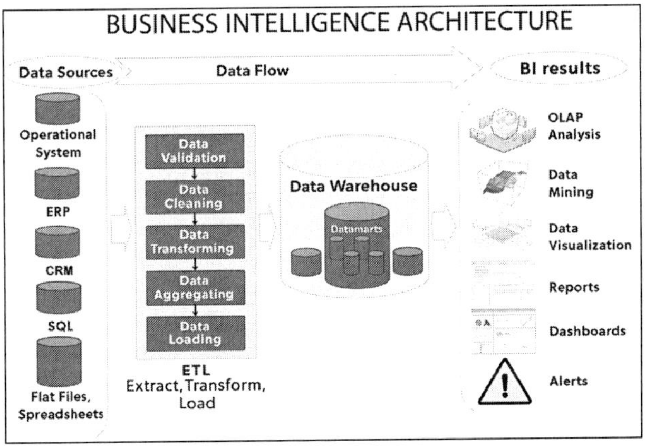

Figure 1.4: *Business Intelligence Architecture and Components*

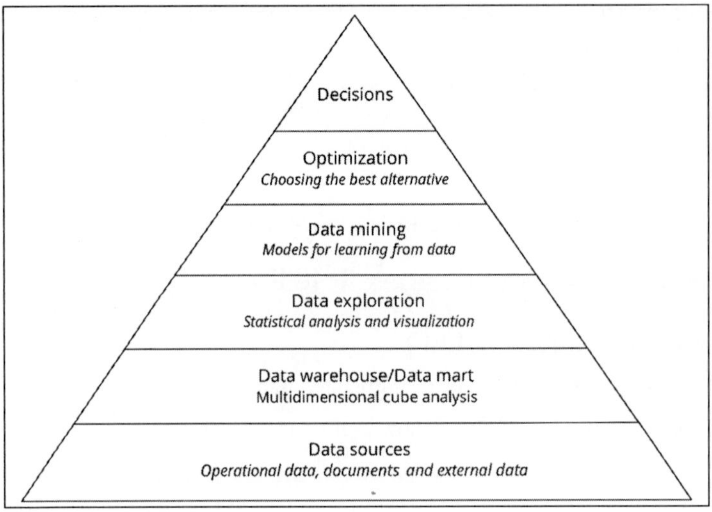

***Figure 1.5:** Business Intelligence Process Layers*

Online Analytical Processing (OLAP)

Online Analytical Processing (OLAP) facilitates multi-faceted business data analysis using an OLAP cube or hypercube, a structure designed for efficient data examination. This cube, composed of numerical facts and dimensions, supports multidimensional queries via operations like Drill-down, Roll-up, Slicing, Dicing, and Pivot, with a data warehouse providing the necessary data foundation through extraction, cleansing, transformation, and loading into the OLAP server.

- **Roll up,** also known as aggregation, condenses data into a more summarized form. This can be done by either decreasing the number of dimensions or by using a concept hierarchy, where data is organized into ordered levels, enabling a high-level view.
- **Drill down** decomposes data into more detailed segments by expanding dimensions within the data cube. This involves moving down a hierarchy or adding new dimensions to the current dataset, allowing for a detailed exploration.
- **Slice and dice** operations extract specific portions of data from the OLAP cube. Slicing selects a single dimension to create a smaller sub-cube, while dicing selects multiple dimensions for a more refined data subset.
- **Pivot** operations change the orientation of the data cube to offer different viewpoints. This rotation allows users to analyze the data from various perspectives, particularly useful when applied to sub-cubes created by slicing, to identify underlying trends and connections.

Data Warehouse

A data warehouse is a specialized database, separate from a company's real-time operational systems, built to support informed decision-making. It integrates cleansed and transformed internal and external data into a structure optimized for analysis. This process, known as data warehousing, empowers decision-makers with accessible and usable information.

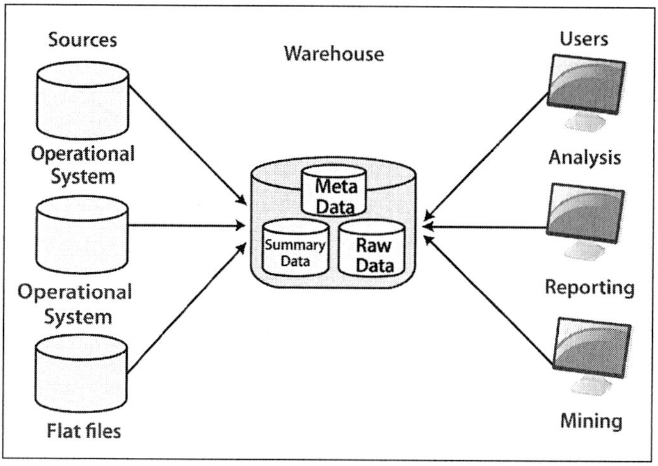

Figure 1.6: Datawarehouse Components Architecture

Operational Systems

Operational systems are the everyday transactional systems that run an organization's core business processes. They serve as the primary source of raw data that is subsequently extracted and loaded into the data warehouse.

Flat Files

Flat files represent a basic method of data storage, where transactional records are stored in individual files, each with a unique identifier. These files are frequently used as a data source for the data warehouse, requiring processing before loading.

Metadata

Metadata, or "data about data," is critical in a data warehouse. It provides descriptive information about the stored data, facilitating easier data discovery, comprehension, and utilization. By summarizing key data attributes, metadata simplifies data management and access.

Lightly and Highly Summarized Data

Data warehouses store pre-calculated summarized data, both lightly and highly aggregated, generated by the warehouse manager. These summaries enable rapid access to key performance indicators and other aggregated metrics, aiding in quick analysis.

End-User Access Tools

End-user access tools are the interfaces that enable business managers to interact with the data warehouse and derive actionable insights. These tools encompass reporting and query tools, application development tools, executive information systems tools, online analytical processing (OLAP) tools, and data mining tools, each catering to different analytical requirements.

ETL (Extract, Transform, Load) Process

The ETL process is the fundamental mechanism for building a data warehouse, orchestrating the movement of data from various sources into a cohesive repository. It requires collaboration from diverse stakeholders and must be adaptable to changing business demands. This recurring, often scheduled, process necessitates agility, automation, and thorough documentation.

Extraction

The initial step, extraction, involves retrieving data from diverse source systems, including relational and NoSQL databases, XML files, and flat files. This extracted data is then temporarily stored in a staging area.

The staging area serves as a critical buffer, as the raw data may contain inconsistencies or errors. This prevents direct loading into the data warehouse, which could compromise its integrity and complicate rollback procedures.

Transformation

The transformation phase focuses on refining the extracted data into a standardized format suitable for the data warehouse. This involves the application of various rules and functions:

- **Filtering:** Selecting only necessary data elements for loading.
- **Cleaning:** Rectifying data inconsistencies, such as substituting default values for nulls or standardizing variations of the same data.
- **Joining:** Merging data from multiple data fields into a single field.
- **Splitting:** Separating a single data field into multiple fields.
- **Sorting:** Arranging data records according to a specified attribute, often a key field.

Loading

The concluding stage, loading, entails transferring the transformed data from the staging area into the data warehouse. The frequency of data loading, whether continuous or periodic, is determined by the specific requirements of the system.

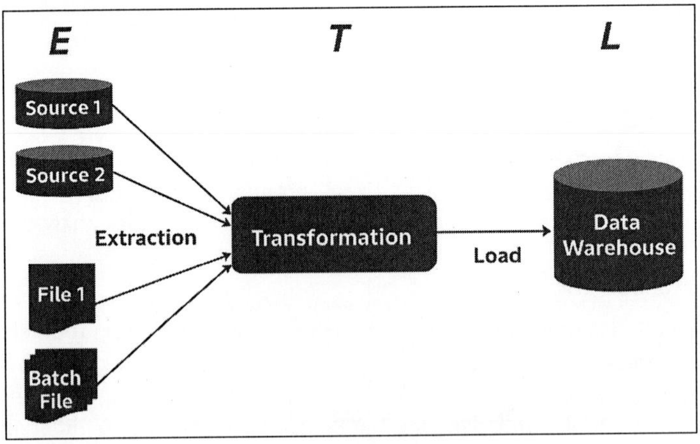

Figure 1.7: *ETL Execution Process*

Business Intelligence Advantages

- **Increased Productivity:** Simplified reporting through BI allows for rapid report generation. This frees up employee time, enabling them to focus on essential tasks and improve overall productivity.
- **Enhanced Visibility:** BI improves process transparency, making it easier to identify areas requiring attention. Data visualization enables businesses to quickly detect bottlenecks and inefficiencies.
- **Strengthened Accountability:** BI systems assign accountability by linking organizational performance to established goals. This ensures individuals are responsible for specific metrics and outcomes.
- **Comprehensive Overview:** BI provides decision-makers with a "bird's-eye view" of organizational performance via dashboards and scorecards. This facilitates rapid identification of trends and patterns.
- **Streamlined Processes:** BI simplifies complex business processes through automated analytics. Predictive analysis, modeling, and benchmarking enable faster, more informed decisions.
- **Accessible Analytics:** BI software has democratized analytics, making it accessible to non- technical users. This empowers a wider range of employees to collect and process data.

Business Intelligence Disadvantages

- **Financial Burden:** Implementing and maintaining BI systems can be expensive, especially for SMEs. Initial investments, ongoing maintenance, and software licensing can strain budgets. **Implementation Complexity:** Data warehouse implementation, a key BI component, can be complex. This complexity can lead to inflexible business processes and hinder adaptability.
- **Limited Accessibility:** Historically, BI solutions were primarily designed for large corporations. This has resulted in limited affordability for many small and medium-sized businesses.

Extended Implementation Time

Data warehousing system implementation can be a lengthy process. This extended timeline can delay the realization of BI benefits.

Business Intelligence Trends

- **AI Integration:** AI and machine learning are being increasingly used in BI. This automates complex data analysis and real-time dashboard reporting. It enables businesses to gain deeper insights and react quickly.
- **Collaborative BI:** BI platforms are incorporating collaboration tools. Features like social media integration facilitate team-based decision-making. This enhances knowledge sharing
- **Embedded BI:** BI functionality is being integrated into other business applications. This improves reporting capabilities and provides seamless access to analytics. Users can access analytics within their existing workflows.

- **Cloud-Based Analytics:** The adoption of cloud-based BI is accelerating. It offers scalability, flexibility, and cost-effectiveness. Cloud analytics adoption is experiencing significant growth.

1.4 BUSINESS QUERY AND REPORTING

Query and Reporting Tools

These tools enable users to access and analyze data for decision-making. They eliminate the need for technical knowledge.

They support both ad-hoc and fixed reports.

- Ad-hoc queries are for one-time questions or exploration.
- Fixed reports are for consistent, recurring data. The process is iterative, with ad-hoc queries potentially becoming fixed reports.

Reporting Software

These tools generate human-readable reports from diverse data sources. They are used for operational reporting and dashboards. Microsoft SQL Server Reporting Services is a leading solution.

Reporting Tool Functionalities

- **Front-End Presentation:** This layer is crucial for effective data presentation. It ensures data is accessible and actionable.
- **Data Source Connectivity:** Reporting tools must connect to various data sources. This includes relational databases and OLAP multidimensional data sources.
- **Scheduling and Distribution:** The ability to schedule report generation and automate distribution is vital. This ensures efficient reporting.
- **Customization Options:** Reporting tools should allow for report customization. This ensures adherence to corporate standards and user preferences.
- **Export Capabilities:** The ability to export reports in common formats is essential. This includes Excel, flat files, and PDF.

Standard Reports

- **Grid Format:** These reports present information in a basic two-dimensional grid. They use rows and columns.
- **Consistent Views:** They provide a consistent, scheduled view of specific business aspects. **Data Representation:** Columns represent measured items or characteristics. Rows represent organizational divisions or hierarchies. The intersection of rows and columns shows specific measurements.

1.5 A BUSINESS VIEW OF THE DATA

Business query tools bridge the gap between technical databases and business users by providing a user-friendly interface. They allow users to access data sources, like data warehouses or operational systems, using business terminology instead of complex SQL queries. A crucial feature is the "business view" or metadata layer, which simplifies the database structure by using familiar business terms and automatically handling table joins and metric calculations (e.g., revenue, customer count). A well-designed business view is essential for accurate queries and avoids overloading reports with excessive logic.

1.6 PRODUCTION REPORTING

Production reporting generates documents like invoices or statements, often directly from transaction systems, operational data stores, or detailed data within a data warehouse. IT departments typically develop these reports to ensure data integrity and prevent resource-intensive queries from untrained users. These reports are often embedded within transaction systems and are designed to meet common, static information needs, such as regulatory compliance.

	Production Reporting	Business Query and Reporting
Primary author	IT developer	Power user or business user
Primary purpose	Document preparation	Decision-making, management
Report delivery	Paper or e-bill, embedded in application	Portal, spreadsheet, e-mail
Print quality	Pixel perfect	Presentation quality
User base	Tens of thousands	Hundreds or thousands
Data source	Operational transaction system	Data warehouse or mart, occasionally transaction system
Level of data detail	Granular	Aggregated
Scope	Operational	Tactical, strategic
Usage	Often embedded within an application	Most often BI as separate application

Microsoft Business Intelligence (MSBI)

MSBI is a suite of tools by Microsoft that provides solutions for business intelligence and data mining. It utilizes Microsoft Visual Studio Data Tools and SQL Server to transform business data into actionable information.

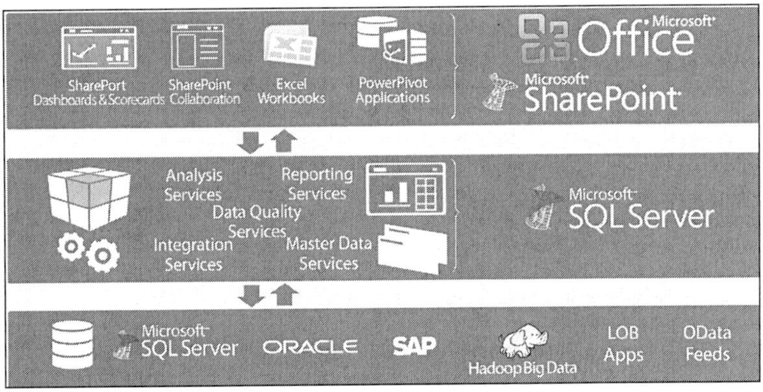

Figure 1.8: MSBI Tools

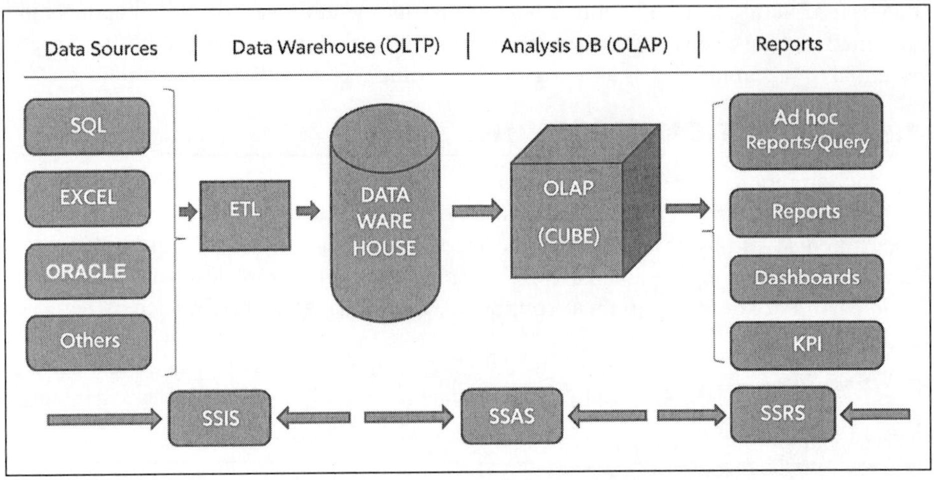

Figure 1.9: Architecture of MSBI

MSBI Tools

- **SQL Server Integration Services (SSIS):** This is Microsoft's ETL tool, used for extracting, transforming, and loading data into data warehouses or data marts. It supports various data sources and formats, allowing for data consolidation. Data warehouses store current and historical data for analysis, while data marts are smaller, focused subsets.
- **SQL Server Analysis Services (SSAS):** SSAS converts two-dimensional (OLTP) data into multidimensional (OLAP) data for advanced analysis. It offers features like multidimensional analysis, KPIs, scorecards, and drill-down capabilities. It also provides good performance and security.

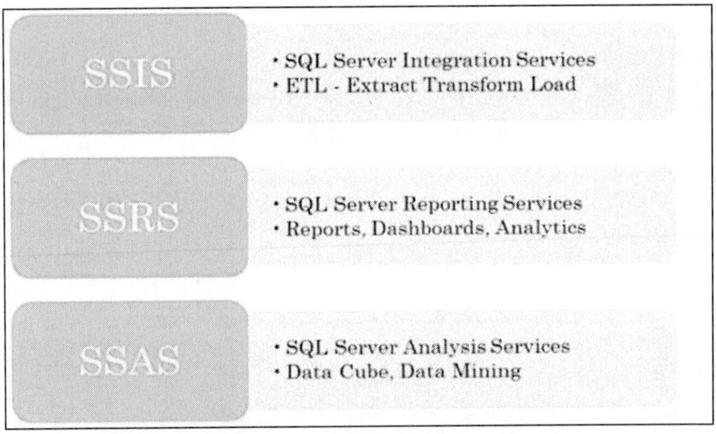

Figure 1.10: Types of MSBI

- **SQL Server Reporting Services (SSRS):** SSRS is an enterprise reporting platform that supports traditional and interactive reports delivered over the web. It can retrieve data from various sources and offers features like ad-hoc reporting and customizable reports. It also provides easy subscription options.

OLTP vs. OLAP

OLTP (Online Transaction Processing)

- Focuses on storing current data for transactional purposes.
- Supports all DML operations (create, read, update, delete).
- Requires high availability.
- Uses normalized databases.
- Data updates frequently.

OLAP (Online Analytical Processing)

- Stores historical and current data from multiple sources for analysis.
- Primarily performs read operations.
- Provides flexible data access.
- Uses denormalized databases for performance.
- Data updates periodically.

OLTP	Business Query and Reporting
Storing the current data (always a production environment)	Storing historical and current data from multiple locations
Perform all DML (create, update, read, delete)	Perform only read
High Availability	Flexible access to data
Normalized database	De-normalized with fewer tables because of less performance with a large volume of data.
Data will update frequently	Periodically update the Data

Data Visualization vs. Data Dashboards

- **Data Visualization:** This refers to the broad practice of representing data in a graphical format.
- Its primary objective is to enhance comprehension and analysis by using visual elements such as charts, graphs, and maps. It focuses on presenting individual data sets in a clear and understandable manner.
- **Data Dashboards:** These are curated collections of related data visualizations, presented in a unified visual layout. They consolidate data from various sources, providing a holistic view of key performance indicators (KPIs) and other relevant metrics. Dashboards are designed for ease of interpretation, particularly for users without technical expertise, often incorporating interactive features for deeper exploration. Their primary purpose is to facilitate monitoring, measurement, and analysis of critical business data.

Creating a Data Dashboard

- **Audience and Goal Definition:** Begin by identifying the intended users of the dashboard and their specific information needs. This understanding will guide the selection of appropriate data and visualizations.

- **Data Selection:** Choose data that directly aligns with the audience's requirements and the dashboard's objectives. Avoid overwhelming users with excessive or irrelevant information.
- **Data Validation:** Ensure the accuracy and cleanliness of the data before building the dashboard. This step is essential to prevent errors and ensure the reliability of insights.
- **Visualization Selection:** Select visualizations that effectively represent the data, considering its complexity. Choose appropriate charts, graphs, or maps to convey the information clearly.
- **Template and Software Utilization:** Utilize templates or user-friendly software to streamline the dashboard creation process. Select a template that aligns with the project's requirements.
- **Simplicity and Consistency:** Maintain visual clarity by using consistent colors, styles, and layouts. Ensure the dashboard is easy to navigate and interpret.
- **Iteration and Refinement:** Gather feedback from the target audience and use it to refine the dashboard. Continuously improve the dashboard's usability and effectiveness.

Types of Data Dashboards

- **Business Dashboards:** Provide summaries of KPIs and key data points. Enable business leaders to monitor team performance and make informed decisions.
- **Executive Dashboards:** Focus on high-level metrics for executive teams. Offer transparency into critical business activities and performance.
- **KPI Dashboards:** Visually display the performance of key data points. Track progress toward specific goals.

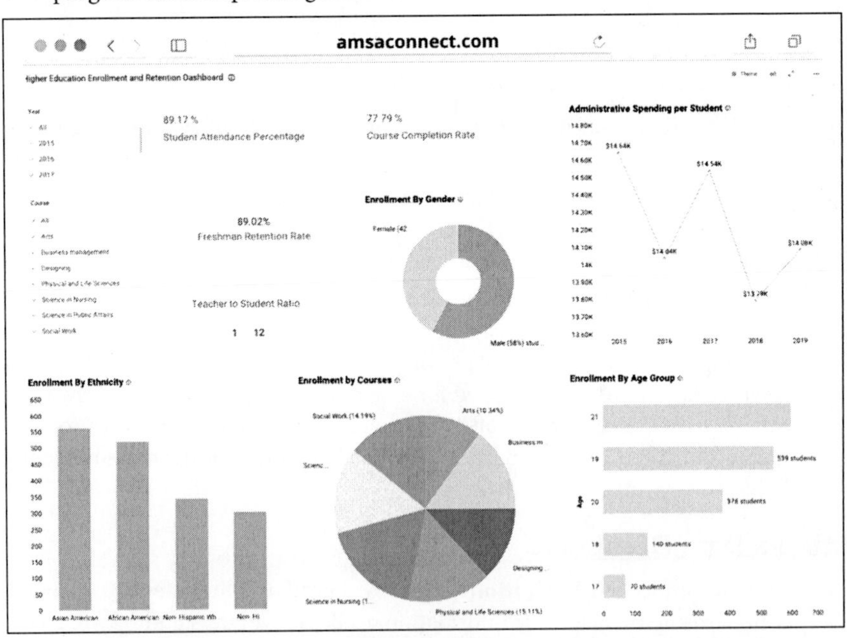

Figure 1.11: Sample Dashboard Template for Educational Application

- **Project Dashboards:** Track project progress and share updates with stakeholders. Provide a comprehensive view of project status and data.
- **Performance Dashboards:** Monitor overall business performance or individual campaign performance. Used across various business functions.
- **Website Dashboards:** Track website performance metrics like traffic, users, and e- commerce activity.
- **Operations Dashboards:** Focus on day-to-day business operations. Provide an end- to-end view of daily activities.
- **Industry-Specific Dashboards:** Tailored to specific industries like healthcare, marketing, and retail. Support decision-making and problem-solving within those industries.
- **Healthcare Dashboards:** Manage critical healthcare data like admission rates, costs, and patient outcomes.
- **Marketing Dashboards:** Track marketing campaign performance and analyze key metrics.
- **Retail Dashboards:** Monitor inventory, sales, and customer engagement.
- **Sales Dashboards:** Track sales performance, leads, and revenue.

Scorecards

A scorecard is a vital tool for performance management, enabling organizations to assess their current activities against planned objectives and desired outcomes. It functions as a strategic alignment tool, tracking key performance indicators (KPIs) related to customer satisfaction, growth, financial health, and operational efficiency. By providing a structured overview, scorecards facilitate the refinement of control mechanisms, the optimization of processes, and the improvement of overall strategic execution.

It's important to note that scorecards typically offer a static, point-in-time view of organizational performance. This characteristic means they are less suitable for dynamic, real-time updates, automated analytical processes, or in-depth, granular investigations of data.

Two Primary Types of Scorecards

Traditional Scorecards: A Departmental Overview

Traditional scorecards offer a simplified, high-level perspective on the performance of individual departments, teams, and employees within an organization.

They are characterized by their straightforward design and reliance on pre-established objectives and metrics.

Key Advantages of Traditional Scorecards

- **Time-Bound Analysis:** They enable the analysis of activities and performance within a defined timeframe, allowing for period-specific evaluations.
- **Performance Evaluation:** They utilize a grading system or defined levels to evaluate performance against set standards.
- **Comparative Analysis:** They facilitate comparisons of performance between individuals, teams, departments, established goals, and historical data, providing valuable context.

Balanced Scorecards: A Holistic Organizational View

- Balanced scorecards provide a comprehensive, multi-dimensional view of an organization's activities, financial standing, and operational performance.
- They integrate data from both external (e.g., market trends, customer feedback) and internal (e.g., financial reports, operational metrics) sources, offering a broad spectrum of insights.
- Key features include the use of critical KPIs, clearly defined goals, and numerical targets to enable easy comparisons and performance tracking.

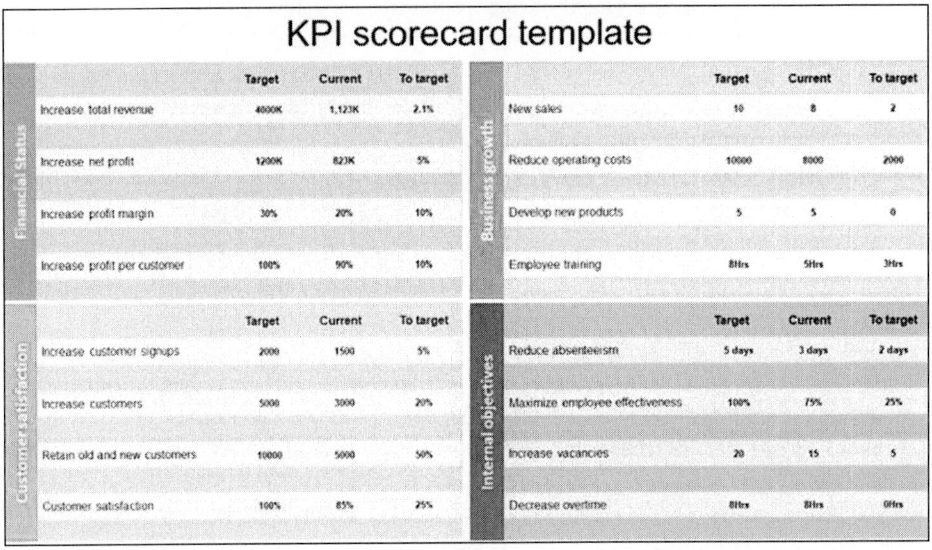

KPI scorecard template

Financial Status	Target	Current	To target
Increase total revenue	4000K	1,123K	2.1%
Increase net profit	1200K	823K	5%
Increase profit margin	30%	20%	10%
Increase profit per customer	100%	90%	10%

Business growth	Target	Current	To target
New sales	10	8	2
Reduce operating costs	10000	8000	2000
Develop new products	5	5	0
Employee training	8Hrs	5Hrs	3Hrs

Customer satisfaction	Target	Current	To target
Increase customer signups	2000	1500	5%
Increase customers	5000	3000	20%
Retain old and new customers	10000	5000	50%
Customer satisfaction	100%	85%	25%

Internal objectives	Target	Current	To target
Reduce absenteeism	5 days	3 days	2 days
Maximize employee effectiveness	100%	75%	25%
Increase vacancies	20	15	5
Decrease overtime	8Hrs	8Hrs	0Hrs

Figure 1.12: *Sample KPI Scorecard Template with differrent phases*

The benefits of balanced scorecards are extensive:

- **Strategic Planning Enhancement:** They aid in the development of robust strategies and the prediction of potential outcomes.
- **Data-Driven Decision-Making:** They promote the use of essential metrics to inform management decisions, ensuring they are grounded in data.
- **Improved Performance Reporting:** They enhance information transparency and streamline KPI management, leading to more effective performance reporting.
- **Progress Monitoring:** They enable the tracking of progress towards established business objectives, ensuring alignment and accountability.
- **Employee Performance Management:** They facilitate the setting of clear performance targets for employees, focusing on outputs and results.
- **Meeting Efficiency:** They reduce the need for unnecessary meetings by providing shared access to performance data.
- **Marketing Effectiveness Analysis:** They aid in identifying the most profitable marketing channels and campaigns.
- **Trend Identification:** They enable the rapid identification of significant trends, allowing for proactive responses.

BI and Analytics

To be classified as an analytic application, according to the International Data Corporation (IDC), software must function independently of its data origins, unify data from diverse sources for time-based examination, automate tasks to refine business operations, and, most importantly, refine a specific operational procedure or industry sector. While dashboards and reports are often included, the distinguishing characteristic of an analytic application is its emphasis on process refinement.

Data Mining and Statistical Analysis: Uncovering Patterns

Data mining and statistical analysis are specialized analytical techniques that employ algorithms to identify trends within datasets. Statisticians typically work with fine-grained (granular) data, while managers tend to utilize summarized (aggregated) data to discern overarching patterns. Data scientists, who are advanced users, utilize a variety of tools, including statistical software, custom SQL queries, programming languages, and BI platforms, to conduct their analyses.

Predictive Analytics: Forecasting the Future

Predictive analytics enable users to develop models, validate them using historical data, and subsequently project future outcomes. Data mining is a crucial component of predictive analysis, and it is also employed in fraud detection, customer segmentation, and market basket analysis. Although predictive analytics represents a distinct area within the broader BI market, it remains a specialized domain, with vendors such as SAS, IBM SPSS, and open-source tools leading the field.

In-Database Analytics: Shifting the Processing Paradigm

Vendors vary in their approaches to the location of analytical processing. Traditionally, statisticians extracted data from source systems and data warehouses to perform analyses outside of the BI environment. However, a growing trend known as "in-database analytics" involves shifting model processing directly into the database. This approach aims to enhance performance and efficiency by leveraging the processing capabilities of the database.

●●●

Intentionally Left Blank!

Business Intelligence Life Cycle

2

UNIT

RATIONALE

Understanding the Business Intelligence (BI) lifecycle is crucial for successful data-driven decision-making. It provides a structured approach, ensuring BI projects align with organizational needs. From analyzing requirements to designing, implementing, and maintaining the system, each phase is vital. This structured process minimizes risks, optimizes resource allocation, and guarantees the BI system delivers actionable insights, ultimately driving business growth and efficiency.

2.1 INTRODUCTION

- **Building a Business Intelligence (BI) System as a Project:** The creation of a BI system can be effectively managed as a project, mirroring the structured approach used in other initiatives. This means it requires a clearly defined end goal, realistic timelines and budgets, and the strategic allocation of resources to execute planned tasks.
- **Analysis:** The initial phase is dedicated to thoroughly understanding the organization's requirements for a BI system. This critical stage involves:
- **Gathering Insights:** Conducting interviews with various employees across different departments to gain a comprehensive understanding of their data needs and workflows.
- **Establishing Objectives:** Clearly outlining the project's overarching goals and priorities.
- **Evaluating Feasibility:** Performing a thorough cost-benefit analysis to justify the investment in the BI system.

2.2 PLANNING

This stage involves detailing the functional capabilities of the BI system. It also includes evaluating existing internal data and potential external data sources. This data assessment allows for the design of the BI architecture's information structures, primarily the central data warehouse and any supporting data marts.

- **Implementation and Control:** The final phase focuses on the construction and ongoing management of the BI system, comprising five distinct sub-phases.
- **Data Warehouse and Data Mart Development:** Constructing the data warehouse and individual data marts, which serve as the data foundations for the BI system. This involves the process of integrating data from various sources.
- **Metadata Management:** Creating a metadata repository to provide context and clarity regarding the data within the data warehouse, including the transformations applied to the original data. This is crucial for data comprehension and accuracy.

- **BI Tool Implementation:** The process of installing and configuring the software used to analyze and report on the data.
- **Testing and Validation:** A rigorous process to ensure the systems functions as intended, and that the data is accurate.
- **Deployment and Training:** The rollout of the system to end users, and the education of those users on how to use the system.

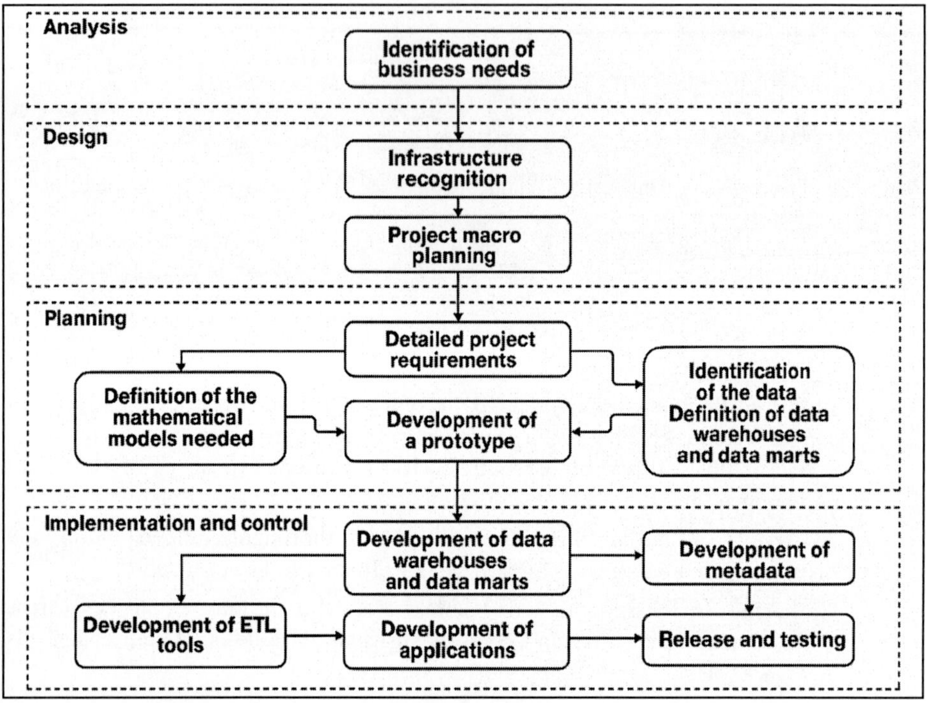

Figure 2.1: *Business Intelligence Life cycle Phases*

2.3 BUSINESS INTELLIGENCE LIFE CYCLE

Business intelligence projects are more time consuming and they require a successful methodology to employ all the business-related operations.

- Understanding the requirements and delivering the valuable business output
- Act in accordance with the proven DW Lifecycle.
- Building and delivering progressively within the organization's data framework
- Designing flexible, useful and high-performance datasets.
- Providing a complete business solution via reports, query tools, documentation.

Program of Project Planning: Laying the Foundation

This is the crucial starting point, where the overall vision and strategy for the BI project are established. It's about ensuring everyone is on the same page and that the project is set up for success.

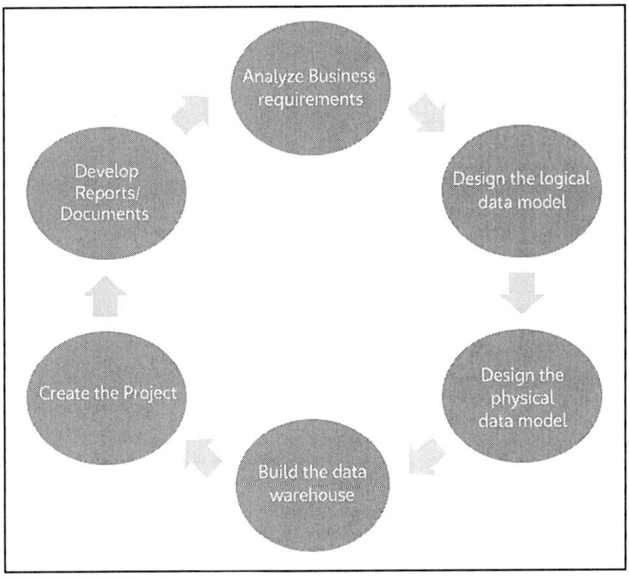

Figure 2.2: Life Cycle of Business Intelligence

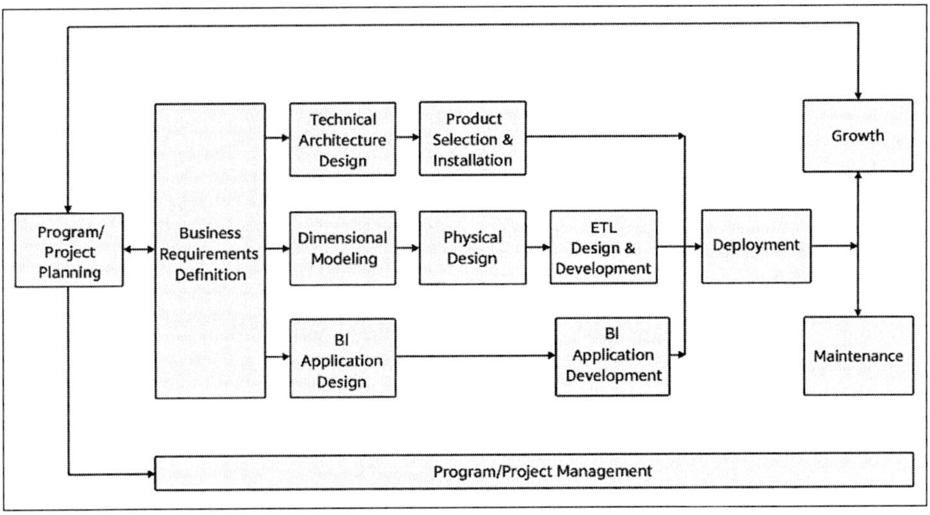

Figure 2.3: Business Life Cycle Architecture

Checklists and Planning Considerations

Business stakeholders, who understand the organization's needs and goals, create detailed checklists. They anticipate potential challenges and develop strategies to mitigate them, particularly in the complex area of data warehousing. Clear roles and responsibilities are defined for each executive involved. This eliminates ambiguity and ensures accountability. Working executives create a comprehensive document that outlines the project's scope, objectives, tasks, timelines, and resources. This plan serves as a roadmap for the entire project. Tasks are prioritized based on their importance and dependencies. This ensures that critical tasks are completed first and that the project stays on schedule. All business requirements are thoroughly analyzed to ensure they are feasible and aligned with the organization's goals. This prevents wasted effort on unrealistic or unnecessary features.

Business Requirements Definition: Translating Needs into Specifications

This phase bridges the gap between the organization's high-level business needs and the specific requirements for the BI system. The project team refines the project plan and estimates the time and resources required for each task. This ensures realistic timelines and budgets. The team considers the project's unique characteristics, such as its cross-functional nature, high visibility, and iterative development. This allows them to tailor the project approach to the specific context. Potential data problems, such as data quality issues or data integration challenges, are identified and addressed early in the process. This prevents costly rework later on. Project plan activities are typically completed within a specific timeframe (e.g., two weeks).

This ensures that the project stays on track and that progress is made consistently. Interviews are conducted with stakeholders and data experts to gather detailed requirements. Comprehensive documentation is created to capture these requirements and ensure that they are clearly understood.

Business Process Dimensional Model (Star Schema): Structuring the Data

The star schema is a simple and intuitive data model that is easy to understand and efficient for querying. This ensures that users can easily access and analyze the data they need. The model consists of dimensions (entities) that represent business concepts (e.g., customers, products, time). Each dimension has attributes that describe its characteristics (e.g., customer name, product category, date). The model is designed to be flexible and adaptable to future changes in business requirements. This ensures that the BI system can evolve with the organization.

BI Application Design: Building the User Interface

User-friendly templates and navigation are designed to make it easy for users to find the information they need. This enhances the user experience and promotes adoption of the BI system. The application includes a range of reporting and analysis tools, such as dashboards, reports, and ad hoc query capabilities. This allows users to perform a variety of analyses and gain insights from the data. The application is designed to facilitate seamless navigation between different reports and analyses.

This ensures that users can easily explore the data and find the information they need. Data validation and performance tuning are performed to ensure that the application is accurate and efficient. This ensures that users can rely on the data and that the application performs well. Security measures are implemented to protect the data. The application is deployed to users, and ongoing maintenance and support are provided. Good documentation is critical.

Growth (Iterative Development): Continuous Improvement

The team regularly reviews the BI system and identifies opportunities for improvement. Priorities are set for future enhancements. Additional dimensions are built to expand the scope of the data model. New BI applications are delivered to meet emerging business needs. Successful processes are rolled out to other parts of the organization. Proven strategies are repeated to maximize the benefits of the BI system. The growth phase leads back to the project planning phase, initiating a new cycle of development. This creates a continuous loop of improvement.

2.4 ENTERPRISE PERFORMANCE LIFE CYCLE (EPLC)

The life cycle stages, stakeholders, performances of various phases and deliverables, exit factors, and project reviews. The EPLC framework is developed to offer the flexibility which is required to effectively handle risk, funds, and profits, while allowing for variations in project size, difficulty, scope, period, and approach. The EPLC framework offers a project management technique that direct the performances of project managers, industry owners, essential partners, IT representatives, and other stakeholders all through the life cycle stages of the project to make sure that a project viewpoint is maintained while scheduling, implementing, and while performing other procedures. Execution of the EPLC framework in a project management is planned to minimize the risk within various projects and along with the investment groups.

2.5 ENTERPRISE PERFORMANCE LIFE CYCLE STAGES

1. Concept Phase

The **Concept** phase marks the initiation of the project, where the primary focus is on identifying the high-level industry and functional needs that will improve the product and deliver value from the planned investment. During this phase, key stakeholders agree on the project's initial benefits, scope, price, plan, and performance metrics. This phase concludes with a preliminary evaluation of project estimates, providing a foundation for further planning and development.

2. Initiation Phase

In the **Initiation** phase, the focus is on identifying the industry requirements, providing rough estimates of project costs and plans, and recognizing potential risks that could impact the project. The outcome is a decision to move forward with a full business case evaluation, a signed project contract, and the creation of an initial project management schedule.

3. Planning Phase

The **Planning** phase is where the project management schedule is fully developed. This phase involves refining the project's cost, plan, and performance baselines and making adjustments as needed. The result is a thorough project plan that clearly outlines the project's needs, scope, and baselines, ensuring the project is well-prepared for execution.

4. Requirements Analysis Phase

The **Requirements Analysis** phase is focused on defining detailed functional and non-functional requirements. A **Requirements Traceability Matrix (RTM)** is created to track the requirements throughout the project lifecycle. The main outcome of this phase is the finalization and approval of requirements, along with any necessary agreements with external partners or vendors.

5. Design Phase

During the **Design** phase, detailed design documents for the product or system are created. These documents serve as the blueprint for development. The outcome of this phase is the successful completion of the product design and the review of both preliminary and detailed design stages, ensuring that the product aligns with the project's objectives.

6. Development Phase

The **Development** phase is where the actual creation of the product takes place, including coding, system configuration, and the development of all essential deliverables. Documentation such as user manuals, operator guides, and security documentation is also created. This phase concludes with the successful completion of coding and test scheduling to ensure the product meets the defined requirements.

7. Test Phase

The **Test** phase involves rigorous testing and auditing of the product's design, code, and documentation to confirm it meets the required specifications. Acceptance testing is performed to ensure the product functions as intended. The phase ends with the completion of acceptance testing and readiness to revise the project plan based on test results and any necessary adjustments.

8. Transition Phase

In the **Transition** phase, user and operator training is conducted to ensure the product is ready for launch. This phase also includes implementing the performance plan to transition the product from development to full production. The result is a smooth transition to full production capacity, along with a post-implementation review to evaluate the project's success and identify areas for improvement.

9. Operations Phase

The **Operations** phase focuses on the ongoing operation of the product. This includes managing the production process and performing annual operational assessments to ensure the product continues to meet performance, cost, and schedule requirements. The outcome is the efficient operation of the product according to the established parameters.

10. Disposition Phase

The **Disposition** phase is the final stage in the lifecycle, during which the product or asset is decommissioned when it is no longer economically viable. This phase involves the systematic withdrawal of the asset, ensuring that information is properly archived and protected as needed. Additionally, lessons learned from the project are documented, and any new assets or operations are smoothly transitioned.

2.6 HUMAN FACTORS IN BUSINESS INTELLIGENCE

Human Factors in BI Implementation refers to abilities, methodologies, equipment's, technology, and customs used to enhance decision making. Therefore, a BI system is known as a decision support system.

Business intelligence will always get synchronized with business data to take resolutions rationally.

As the duration of business is growing, a variety of business intelligence solutions are getting introduced. Every successful business intelligence execution, irrespective of the volume and capacity, must deal with how the project is influenced by human factors. Greatest possible procedures can be assembled and acquire high operate software and infrastructure machineries.

Human Factors in BI Implementation

To ensure a successful BI rollout, organizations must prioritize aligning the system with actual business operations, rather than solely focusing on technical capabilities. A demonstrable return on investment (ROI) is achieved through a well- crafted business case, the establishment of clear key performance indicators (KPIs), and continuous monitoring against defined benchmarks. A competent and dedicated project manager is indispensable for fostering team synergy and driving project momentum. Strong executive sponsorship, extending beyond management to include the CEO and senior leadership, provides critical support and direction. Proactive planning, which entails scheduling key events early in the project, minimizes the need for reactive problem-solving later on. Comprehensive training and change management initiatives are essential for equipping users with the skills and knowledge to effectively utilize the BI system, thereby enhancing user adoption and maximizing its overall value.

BI Strategy Fundamentals

A comprehensive BI strategy acts as a structured plan, outlining the optimal blend of processes and technologies to achieve an organization's strategic intelligence goals. It guarantees the delivery of dependable and pertinent information, facilitating effective business performance management through a combination of established and innovative techniques. Contrary to popular misconceptions, BI is not limited to a data warehouse, OLAP tool, dashboard, or specific technology; it is a comprehensive, enterprise-wide system that leverages current and reliable data to support performance management and informed decision-making. BI empowers business users to access, analyze, and distribute information, thereby assuming an increasingly strategic role as organizations seek to extract valuable insights from their operational data. Developing a BI roadmap that is closely aligned with business goals enables the full realization of data's potential, while benchmarking BI maturity against industry peers and tailoring the roadmap to both current and future objectives ensures a competitive edge.

Objectives and Deliverables of BI

The core objectives of a well-defined BI strategy include establishing a single, authoritative source of information, promoting data-driven decision- making over subjective opinions. Data alignment across the organization fosters a cohesive company strategy, while readily accessible information streamlines the prioritization of impact analysis. Thorough evaluations, delivering reliable, accurate, and timely insights, empower organizations to effectively measure performance. "What-if" scenario analysis supports informed decision-making, and the capability to consistently define and measure KPIs across all divisions enhances organizational performance management. Establishing a comprehensive information dissemination network ensures that insights are effectively communicated throughout the enterprise.

Building a BI Transformation Roadmap

A BI transformation roadmap articulates the guiding principles for developing the planned BI architecture and its supporting technologies. It commences with a high-level overview, with detailed specifications added as the development progresses. This roadmap should establish governance frameworks and procedures, define conceptual, logical, and physical architectures, map infrastructure dependencies, create information delivery projects, and specify comprehensive information requirements. It must consider the informational needs of customers, including their preferred data access and usage methods, and address crucial aspects such as capability, performance, data efficiency, security, metadata control, and data maintenance.

The roadmap should also integrate a BI performance timeline, project prioritization criteria, and resource availability, while a broad policy framework summarizes the transformation and guides future operational processes. For instance, high-level decisions regarding data maintenance will significantly impact data architecture and methodological design.

2.7 BI DEVELOPMENT STAGES AND STEPS

Stage 1. Justification

This initial phase focuses on determining the driving force behind a new BI engineering project. It involves a thorough assessment of the business needs that necessitate the project, ensuring a clear understanding of its purpose and potential value.

Stage 2. Planning

Here, strategic and tactical plans are formulated, outlining the comprehensive approach to the BI engineering project's execution and deployment. These plans serve as a roadmap, guiding the project's progress and ensuring alignment with organizational objectives.

Stage 3. Business Analysis

This stage entails a detailed analysis of the business problem or opportunity, aiming to gain a deep understanding of the business requirements for a potential BI solution. The focus is on translating business needs into actionable specifications.

Stage 4. Design

The design phase involves conceptualizing a BI product that effectively addresses the identified business problem or capitalizes on the business opportunity. This stage focuses on creating a blueprint for the solution.

Stage 5. Construction

This is the build phase, where the BI product is developed, aiming to deliver a return on investment within a predetermined timeframe. The focus is on creating a functional and valuable solution.

Stage 6. Deployment

This phase involves implementing or launching the finished BI product, followed by a thorough evaluation of its effectiveness. This assessment determines whether the solution meets, exceeds, or falls short of the expected return on investment.

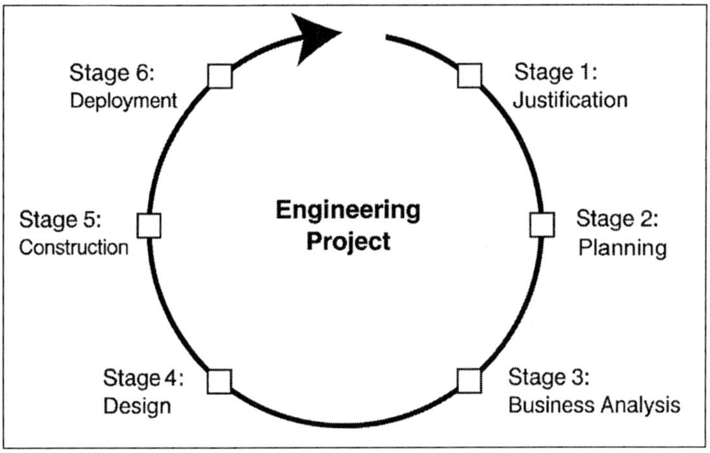

Figure 2.4: *Engineering Development Stages*

Project Refinement

Following the deployment stage, the project enters a refinement cycle. This involves incorporating user feedback and addressing any identified defects, leading to continuous improvement.

Phase 1: Justification

Step 1: Business Case Development

- Clearly define the pressing business problem or promising opportunity that necessitates a BI solution.
- Present specific BI solutions, each with a detailed cost-benefit analysis, demonstrating the tangible value of addressing the identified need.

Phase 2: Planning

Step 2: Infrastructure Assessment

- Acknowledge the cross-organizational nature of BI, requiring a robust enterprise infrastructure.
- Evaluate existing technical infrastructure (hardware, software, databases, networks) and non-technical infrastructure (standards, data models, methodologies).
- Identify gaps and plan for necessary development.

Step 3: Project Blueprinting

- Recognize the dynamic nature of BI projects and potential changes in scope, budget, and technology.
- Develop a detailed project plan with clear monitoring and reporting mechanisms.

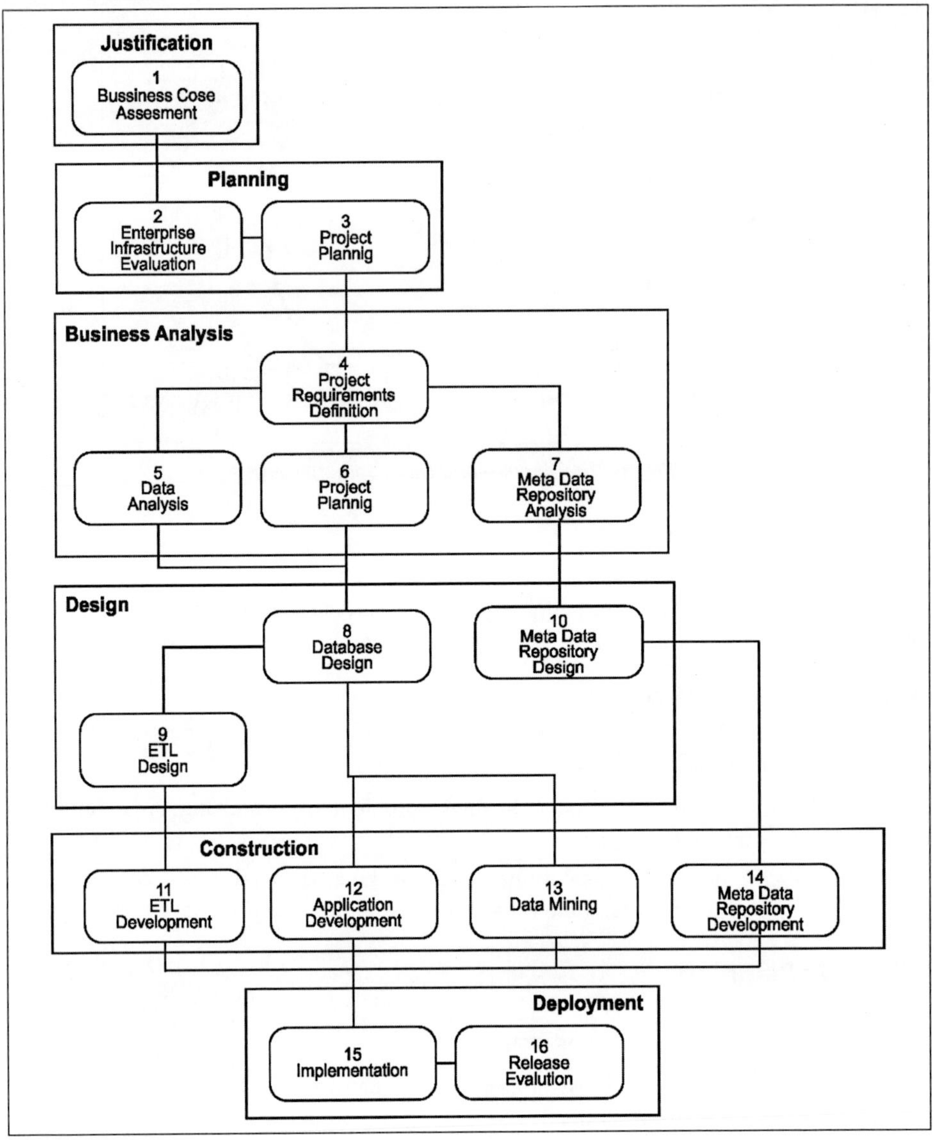

Figure 2.5: *Business Intelligence Development Steps*

Phase 3: Business Analysis

Step 4: Requirements Definition

- Collaboratively define project deliverables, anticipating evolving requirements as stakeholders gain deeper BI technology understanding.

Step 5: Data Quality Assessment

- Address data quality as a primary challenge, overcoming historical data silos and ensuring cross-organizational data reconciliation.

Step 6: Prototype Development

- Use prototyping to analyze functionality, validate concepts, and provide stakeholders with hands-on experience, enabling requirement adjustments.

Step 7: Metadata Analysis

- Map technical and business metadata, store it in a central repository, and document metadata capture requirements in a logical model.

Phase 4: Design

Step 8: Database Architecture

- Design the BI database to accommodate both detailed and aggregated data, aligning with reporting requirements.

Step 9: ETL Design

- Analyze source data to identify gaps, define relationships, and establish ETL procedures.

Step 10: Metadata Repository Design

- Design the metadata repository (entity-relationship or object-oriented) to meet the logical metadata model's requirements.

Phase 5: Construction

Step 11: ETL Implementation

- Implement ETL processes to extract, transform, and load data into the BI database.

Step 12: Application Development

- Develop the BI application, using the populated database to create operational prototypes, often concurrently with ETL and metadata repository development.

Step 13: Data Mining Implementation

- Utilize data mining tools to uncover hidden insights beyond standard reports.

Step 14: Metadata Repository Development

- Develop a custom metadata repository if a licensed solution is not preferred.

Phase 6: Deployment Step 15: System Launch

- Deploy the tested BI system and initiate support functions, including help desk, database maintenance, and ETL job scheduling.

Step 16: Post-Implementation Review

- Conduct a review to capture lessons learned, analyze deviations, and refine processes for future releases.

Parallel Development Tracks

Imagine building a house. You wouldn't wait for the foundation to be completely finished before starting on the walls, right? Similarly, in complex BI projects, we use parallel development tracks to work on different components simultaneously, saving time and resources.

Why Parallel Tracks?

BI projects involve many interconnected parts: getting data ready, building the user interface, and managing metadata. Working on these sequentially would take a very long time. Parallel tracks allow teams to work concurrently, making the project more efficient.

The Three Key Tracks

ETL Track (Back End)

This is the "data preparation" track. It's about extracting data from various sources, cleaning it, transforming it into a usable format, and loading it into the data warehouse. Think of it as the kitchen staff preparing all the ingredients before the chef starts cooking. This track is crucial because the quality of your BI system depends on the quality of your data.

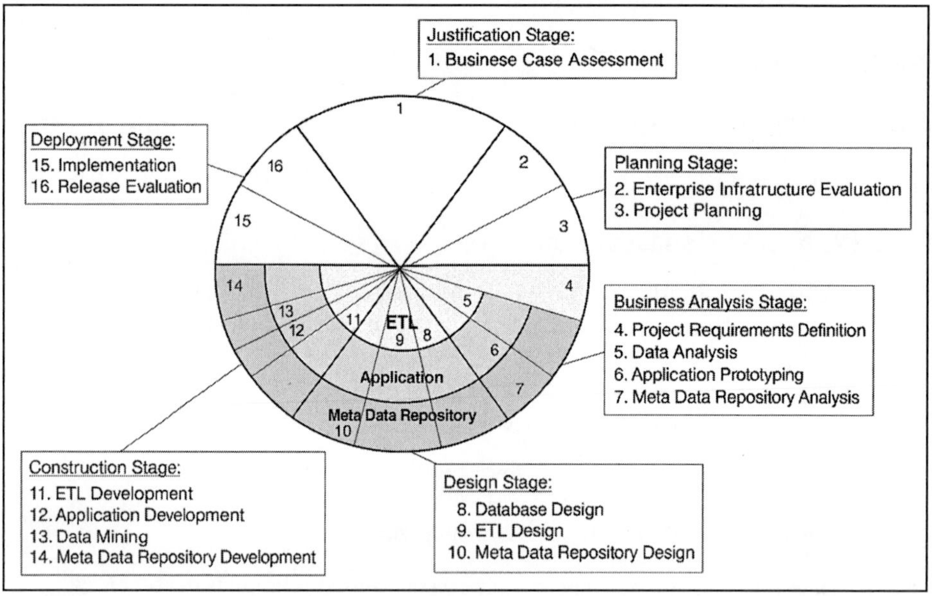

Figure 2.6: Parallel Development Tracks

Application Track (Front End)

This is the "user experience" track. It's about building the tools and interfaces that users will interact with, like dashboards, reports, and query tools. Think of it as designing the dining room and creating the menu. This track focuses on making the data accessible and easy to understand for business users.

Meta Data Repository Track

This is the "data documentation" track. It's about creating a central repository that stores information about the data itself, like its source, meaning, and transformations. Think of it as creating a detailed index and glossary for all your data. This track helps users understand the data and ensures consistency across the BI system.

BI Framework: A Structured Approach to BI

A BI framework is like a recipe for successful BI. It provides a structured approach to managing BI activities, ensuring that data is used effectively to support decision-making.

Why a Framework?

Without a framework, BI projects can become chaotic and disorganized. A framework provides a roadmap, ensuring that all aspects of BI are considered.

Benefits of a Framework

- **Improved Data Quality:** Ensures data is accurate and consistent.
- **Enhanced Accuracy of Insights:** Leads to more reliable and trustworthy analysis. **Actionable Reporting:** Creates reports that are easy to understand and use for decision- making.

●●●

Intentionally Left Blank!

Business Intelligence User Model

3

UNIT

RATIONALE

The Business Intelligence (BI) User Model refers to the categorization of users within a BI system based on their roles, needs, and interaction with data. It identifies different user types such as data analysts, executives, and operational staff, each with varying levels of access to data, tools, and reports. The model helps tailor BI solutions to meet the specific requirements of different user groups, improving decision-making and data accessibility across the organization.

3.1 STAGES OF EVOLUTION OF BUSINESS INTELLIGENCE

The 1980's – printed green bar reports During the late 1970s and early 1980s, the concept of Decision Support Systems (DSS) Evolved from two previous types of computer support for decision making.

One was a Management Information System (MIS), which provided:

1. Scheduled reports for well-defined information needs
2. Demand reports for ad hoc information requests
3. The ability to query a database for specific data
    - In the 1980's, the task for business intelligence was to print green bar reports from dot matrix printers.
    - In the 1990's, business intelligence transitioned to OLAP (Online Analysis Processing) and ROLAP (Relational Online Analytical Processing).
    - Warehousing and cubes concepts were introduced; users had the capability to use those cubes to manage departmental data in separate cubes.
    - Users could also run queries directly to relational databases, which were the ROLAP model.
    - In the early 2000's, Web-based business intelligence was introduced for the first time.
    - Users could finally have access to real-time consumption of information. Users could run reports through a Web-based application and make charts and graphs to give a graphical look to reports.
    - Late 2000's, dashboards were finally built. Users moved away from grids and graphs of 50-page reports and finally got into the Consumable dashboards that business users can use to view data at a glance and see what is going on in the business.
    - In the 2010's, the trend is in portable and swift business intelligence, which is also called mobile business intelligence.

- Portable and swift business intelligence basically is taking all the business intelligence that has been created in the past and integrating it into mobile devices for consumption and also enabling visual data discovery for casual business users.

3.2 TYPES OF BUSINESS INTELLIGENCE TOOLS AND APPLICATIONS

Ad hoc analysis also known as ad hoc querying

1. Online analytical processing (OLAP).
2. Mobile BI. (Mobile business intelligence).
3. Real-time BI.
4. Operational intelligence (OI).
5. Software-as-a-service BI (SaaS BI).
6. Open source BI (OSBI).
7. Embedded BI.
8. Collaborative BI.
9. Location intelligence (LI).

3.3 CONTENT MANAGEMENT SYSTEM (CMS)

A Content Management System (CMS) is a software application designed to facilitate the creation, editing, modification, organization, and deletion of content from a centralized interface. CMS platforms were introduced in the late 1990s and are widely used to manage websites, including blogs, news platforms, and e-commerce sites. These systems are designed to simplify content management, eliminating the need for manual coding.

CMS Components

- **Database (ODBC SQL):** Stores content and metadata used by the CMS.
- **Middleware Language:** Tools like PHP, ASP, and frameworks such as Django and Drupal that help execute the backend logic.
- **Administrative Layer:** Handles user management, authorizations, logins, and access rights.
- **Approval System:** Ensures content passes through an approval process before being published.
- **Workflow System:** Defines the sequence of steps and user roles involved in content creation and approval.
- **Business Logic Layer:** Implements scripts and programs that tailor content delivery to specific user groups.
- **Presentation Layer:** Uses technologies like HTML, CSS, JavaScript, and AJAX to format and display content for end users.

Types of CMS

- **Enterprise Content Management System (ECMS):** An advanced CMS with features to manage a wider array of organizational information, such as document and record management, digital assets, and collaborative tools.

- **Document Management System (DMS):** Focuses on managing the creation, storage, and flow of documents in an organization. DMSs offer centralized repositories and metadata to organize and track documents.
- **Records Management System (RMS):** Manages records, both physical and electronic, and ensures they are captured, maintained, and accessible over time.
- **Digital Asset Management (DAM):** Specializes in managing multimedia content, like images, videos, and audio. DAM systems offer functionalities like storage, retrieval, and rights management for digital assets.
- **Brand Management Systems:** A specific type of DAM focused on managing marketing and promotional materials used for brand advertising.
- **Digital Imaging System (DIMS):** Automates the creation of digital versions of paper documents, such as PDFs, and integrates with records management systems.
- **Learning Management System (LMS):** Automates the administration of training programs, handling tasks like registration, resource management, and tracking results.
- **Learning Content Management System (LCMS):** Combines features of a CMS and LMS to manage both training content and the administrative aspects of educational courses.
- **Geographic Information Systems (GIS):** Specialized systems for managing spatial data, used for capturing, storing, retrieving, analyzing, and displaying location-based information.

3.4 HEADLESS CMS VS. TRADITIONAL CMS

- **Traditional CMS (Coupled CMS)** refers to a content management system where both the backend (content management) and the frontend (presentation layer) are integrated into a single system. In this setup, the system is often designed to manage and display content on a specific webpage. The CMS controls both content creation and its layout, making it suitable for projects where the content is presented mainly on web pages. This architecture is typically page-based and can limit flexibility, as everything from content management to display is tightly coupled.
- **Headless CMS** is an advanced form of content management where the backend (content management) is decoupled from the frontend (content presentation). In a headless CMS, the content is stored and managed in the backend, and developers can use APIs to send content to any platform or device, such as mobile apps, websites, or IoT devices. This architecture allows greater flexibility and scalability as the content can be reused across multiple channels and devices without being tied to a specific layout or presentation format.

3.5 END USER SEGMENTATION

User segmentation is the practice of dividing users into different groups, or segments, based on shared characteristics or behaviors. This process allows businesses to better understand their customers, customize their offerings, and create targeted marketing strategies. Segmentation can be done based on factors like language preferences, geographic region, product usage, or user persona (such as age, occupation, interests). An end user is a person who interacts with or uses a product or service. They are the final consumers of the product, whether it's a software application, physical product, or service. Segmentation is crucial because it helps companies tailor their products and services more effectively. It's not just about categorizing people but about gaining a deeper understanding of customer needs, preferences, and behaviors to improve user experience, optimize product offerings, and enhance marketing efforts.

3.6 CUSTOMER SEGMENTATION MODELS

1. Demographic Segmentation
2. Geographic Segmentation
3. Psychographic Segmentation
4. Technographic Segmentation
5. Behavioral Segmentation
6. Needs-based Segmentation
7. Value-based Segmentation

1. Demographic Segmentation

This model divides customers based on their demographic characteristics such as age, gender, income, education level, occupation, and family size. It's one of the most common types of segmentation and helps businesses target specific groups based on their basic social and economic traits.

2. Geographic Segmentation

Geographic segmentation involves dividing customers based on their location. This can include region, country, city, climate, or even population density. It's useful for businesses looking to tailor their products or services to specific geographic areas, considering factors like local preferences or regional needs.

3. Psychographic Segmentation

Psychographic segmentation goes deeper into understanding customers' lifestyles, values, interests, attitudes, and personality traits. It helps businesses target customers based on their psychological and emotional characteristics, rather than just demographic information. This model is effective for creating more personalized and emotionally appealing marketing strategies.

4. Technographic Segmentation

Technographic segmentation categorizes customers based on their technology usage. It examines factors like the type of devices, software, or tools customers use. This model is particularly relevant for businesses in the tech industry, helping them understand customer needs based on their technological behaviors and preferences.

5. Behavioral Segmentation

Behavioral segmentation focuses on customers' behaviors, including their purchasing patterns, product usage, brand loyalty, and response to marketing efforts. By analyzing how customers interact with a product or service, businesses can segment them into groups like frequent buyers, occasional users, or those who are likely to churn.

6. Needs-based Segmentation

This segmentation model divides customers based on their specific needs and problems. It helps businesses understand what drives customer decisions and what particular requirements they have. It's highly useful for businesses offering complex products or services where customers have distinct functional needs.

7. Value-based Segmentation

Value-based segmentation categorizes customers based on the value they bring to a business. This could be determined by factors like the customer's profitability, lifetime value, or purchasing potential. It allows businesses to prioritize high-value customers and tailor marketing efforts to retain them, often with personalized offers or premium services.

3.7 CUSTOMER SEGMENTATION STRATEGY

A Customer Segmentation Strategy is a plan used by businesses to categorize their customer base into specific groups or segments based on shared traits, behaviors, or needs. The primary goal is to customize products, services, and marketing efforts to align with the unique characteristics of each segment. By doing so, businesses can enhance customer satisfaction, boost conversion rates, and drive revenue growth.

Here's a comprehensive guide on the key elements involved in a customer segmentation strategy:

1. Identifying Customer Segments

The first step is to identify the various customer groups within your target market. This involves gathering and analyzing data to detect patterns in behaviors, preferences, and other defining factors. Depending on business objectives, segmentation can be based on various models, such as:

- **Demographic Segmentation**: Factors like age, gender, and income.
- **Geographic Segmentation**: Grouping based on location.
- **Psychographic Segmentation**: Segmenting based on lifestyle, values, and interests.
- **Behavioral Segmentation**: Based on consumer purchasing behavior, loyalty, and usage.
- **Needs-based Segmentation**: Focusing on specific needs or pain points.

2. Analyzing Data and Defining Segments

After collecting data, the next step is to analyze it to create actionable customer segments. Using data analytics tools, machine learning, or customer relationship management (CRM) systems, businesses can group customers based on shared characteristics or behaviors.

For example:

- A business may find that younger consumers (18-24) prefer online shopping and prioritize convenience.

- On the other hand, older consumers (45+) may value personalized services and loyalty rewards.

By examining customer behaviors, past purchases, or social media interactions, businesses can spot trends and establish meaningful customer segments.

3. Creating Customer Personas

Once the segments are identified, businesses should develop **customer personas**—fictional profiles that represent the ideal customer for each segment. These personas typically include:

- **Demographic details**: Age, income, location, etc.
- **Buying behavior**: Purchase frequency, preferred products, etc.
- **Pain points**: The challenges or issues they are trying to solve.
- **Goals and motivations**: What drives them to make purchasing decisions.

Creating these personas helps businesses better understand their target audience and craft marketing strategies that resonate with each segment.

4. Developing Tailored Marketing and Product Strategies

With clear customer segments and personas, businesses can develop targeted approaches to engage each group effectively. Here's how segmentation can shape marketing and product strategies:

- **Product Customization**: Tailor products to meet the specific needs of each group. For instance, a skincare brand could create anti-aging solutions for older customers and acne treatments for younger ones.
- **Pricing Strategies**: Different segments may have varying price sensitivities. High- income segments may prefer premium products, while budget-conscious customers may respond better to discounts or special offers.
- **Personalized Marketing**: Businesses can create targeted marketing campaigns that speak directly to each segment's interests and preferences. For example, an email campaign could offer personalized discounts based on past purchases.
- **Channel Selection**: Different segments may prefer different communication channels. Younger audiences may prefer social media, while older customers might engage more with email newsletters or in-store experiences.

5. Enhancing Customer Service and Experiences

Customer segmentation also plays a key role in shaping how businesses provide customer service:

- **VIP Customers**: High-value or loyal customers may receive priority service, exclusive offers, or dedicated account managers.
- **Frequent Shoppers**: Businesses can offer loyalty rewards or personalized promotions to retain regular buyers.

By tailoring the customer experience based on segmentation, businesses can improve satisfaction and foster long-term customer relationships.

6. Ongoing Monitoring and Optimization

Customer segmentation is a dynamic process. As customer preferences and market trends evolve, businesses need to continuously assess and refine their segmentation strategies.

This involves:

- **Gathering feedback** from customers through surveys or reviews.
- **Analyzing shifts** in customer behaviors and market conditions.
- **Testing and refining** marketing campaigns to ensure they remain effective for each segment.

Tools like A/B testing, customer journey mapping, and analytics can help businesses assess how well their segmentation strategy is performing and make necessary adjustments.

7. Measuring Success and ROI

To evaluate the effectiveness of a segmentation strategy, businesses must track and measure key performance indicators (KPIs), such as:

- **Customer Acquisition and Retention Rates**: How effectively is the strategy attracting new customers and retaining existing ones?
- **Conversion Rates**: Are customers responding positively to targeted offers and campaigns?
- **Customer Lifetime Value (CLV)**: Are the segmented groups contributing to long-term business growth?
- **Customer Satisfaction**: Are customers pleased with the tailored experiences and offerings?

Advantages of Customer Segmentation

Customer segmentation provides numerous benefits for businesses, enabling them to understand their customers more deeply, refine their marketing strategies, and foster growth. Here are the key advantages:

1. Enhanced Targeting and Personalization

Segmenting customers into distinct groups allows businesses to create tailored marketing campaigns, product suggestions, and promotions that resonate with each specific segment. This approach increases customer engagement and conversion rates, as individuals feel that the brand addresses their individual needs.

2. Improved Marketing Efficiency

Segmentation enables businesses to allocate marketing resources more effectively. Instead of delivering broad, generic messages to everyone, companies can focus their marketing efforts on the segments most likely to respond. This increases the return on investment (ROI) by minimizing waste and boosting effectiveness.

3. Stronger Customer Retention

By meeting the unique needs of each customer segment, businesses can develop stronger, more lasting relationships with their audience. Offering personalized experiences, loyalty programs, and relevant content helps boost customer satisfaction and loyalty, which in turn drives repeat business and enhances retention.

4. Higher Revenue and Profit Margins

Identifying and prioritizing high-value customer segments enables businesses to concentrate on the most profitable groups. Tailored offers and products that address the specific needs of each segment can increase sales, raise average order values, and ultimately improve profitability.

5. Better Product Innovation and Development

By understanding the unique challenges, preferences, and needs of different customer groups, businesses can create products and services that are more closely aligned with customer expectations. This leads to more successful product launches and better-targeted innovations that appeal directly to specific market segments.

6. Enhanced Customer Experience

Customer segmentation allows businesses to provide a more personalized experience, whether through customized communications, product offerings, or support services. A more tailored customer experience fosters greater satisfaction, increases loyalty, and strengthens the long-term success of the business.

7. Competitive Edge

Having a deeper understanding of customer segments gives businesses an edge over competitors. By adapting their products, services, and messaging to meet the distinct needs of different groups, companies can differentiate themselves and create more attractive offerings for their target segments.

8. Effective Resource Management

Segmentation helps businesses allocate resources where they are most needed. Marketing budgets can be targeted at the most lucrative segments, and staffing, inventory, and product development can be optimized to align with the preferences and needs of specific customer groups.

9. Tailored Communication Strategies

Segmentation enables businesses to choose the best communication channels for different customer groups. Younger audiences might prefer social media, while older customers may engage better through email or in-person interactions. Customizing communication strategies improves engagement and boosts response rates.

10. Improved Forecasting and Analysis

Customer segmentation allows businesses to better understand trends, behaviors, and demands within specific segments. This leads to more accurate sales forecasting, demand planning, and market analysis. Knowing which segments contribute most to growth enables businesses to make more informed strategic decisions and investments.

3.8 BENEFITS OF ANALYZING YOUR CUSTOMER SEGMENTATION

- Improve product delivery.
- Boost process efficiency.
- Help you target content marketing and sales outreach.
- Update pricing, plans, and strategy.
- Improve customer relationships.

- Create new offers, products, and services.
- Improve brand awareness.
- Stay ahead of competitors.
- Track product sentiment.

3.9 ONLINE ANALYTICAL PROCESSING (OLAP)

Let's break down Online Analytical Processing (OLAP) in a way that's easy to understand and avoids repeating the exact phrasing. Imagine you're trying to understand your company's sales performance. Instead of looking at flat spreadsheets, OLAP lets you explore the data from many angles, like turning a Rubik's Cube. The core idea is multidimensional analysis. Think of your data as living inside a cube. Each side of the cube represents a different aspect, like:

- **Time:** Years, quarters, months, days
- **Location:** Regions, countries, cities
- **Products:** Categories, brands, individual items

This cube is called an OLAP cube. It's built to store your data in a way that makes it incredibly fast to answer complex questions. Before you even ask, the system has already calculated many of the answers, storing pre-aggregated results. This pre-calculation is a key reason for the speed of OLAP.

Now, let's say you want to explore your sales data. You can use several operations:

- **"Roll-up" is like summarizing.** You might start by looking at total sales for the year, and then "roll up" to see sales for the entire company.
- **"Drill-down" is the opposite.** You could start with yearly sales and "drill down" to see how each month performed.
- **"Slice" is like taking a single page from a book.** You could look at sales for a specific region during a specific month.
- **"Dice" lets you select a smaller chunk of the cube.** For example, sales of a specific product category within a specific region and time period.
- **"Pivot" is like rotating the cube.** You could switch from viewing sales by region to viewing sales by product.

There are a Few Ways to Build these OLAP Systems

- **MOLAP (Multidimensional):** This is like having a specialized, super-fast database built just for OLAP. It pre-calculates everything and stores it in the cube.
- **ROLAP (Relational):** This uses your existing relational database (like those used for everyday transactions) and translates your OLAP queries into standard database queries. It's flexible but can be slower.
- **HOLAP (Hybrid):** This is a mix of both. It might store the most frequently used data in a specialized cube and keep the rest in the relational database.

Why is OLAP so Valuable?

It's a crucial tool for business intelligence, helping companies understand their data and spot trends. It empowers decision-makers to quickly get the information they need. It supports data mining by making it easier to find hidden patterns. It simplifies the creation of reports that are clear and interactive. In essence, OLAP transforms raw data into actionable insights, enabling faster and more informed business decisions.

3.10 ADVANCED/EMERGING BI TECHNOLOGIES

We're diving into the future of Business Intelligence (BI), where data analysis transcends basic reports and delivers deeper, more interactive insights.

BI's Continuous Growth

BI is a dynamic field, constantly improving to make data more accessible and understandable. This includes:

- **Advanced Visualizations:** Moving beyond simple charts to create dynamic, visually compelling data representations, revealing complex patterns.
- **Expanding Data Access:** Empowering more users across the organization with data-driven insights.

Evaluating New BI Tools

While numerous new BI technologies emerge, businesses must prioritize tools that effectively address their specific needs.

Key Advancements in BI

- **Visual Data Storytelling:** Transforming raw data into clear, insightful visuals for faster trend identification and informed decision-making.
- **Intelligent Analytical Guidance:** Providing proactive assistance through guided workflows and automated alerts, enabling users to navigate complex analyses efficiently. For instance, triggering alerts and providing guided troubleshooting when key performance indicators decline.
- **Pattern Discovery through Data Mining:** Analyzing large datasets to uncover hidden trends and correlations, providing valuable insights for predicting future outcomes. Leveraging increased digital data storage for more comprehensive analysis.
- **Extracting Insights from Unstructured Data:** Analyzing diverse data formats like emails and social media to gain actionable business intelligence. Enabling businesses to understand customer sentiment and extract valuable information from various sources.

3.11 FUTURE OF BUSINESS INTELLIGENCE

AI and machine learning are making BI more powerful. Think predictions, automated data cleanup, finding hidden connections, and even talking to your data using plain language. Cloud-based BI means easier scaling, flexibility, and cost savings. You get real-time access from anywhere, smoother integration with different data sources, and better teamwork. Businesses need to know what's happening *now*. Real-time analytics let them monitor data as it arrives, react quickly to changes, and keep operations running smoothly. BI is getting more engaging with interactive dashboards, data storytelling, and even AR/VR visualizations. This makes complex data easier for everyone to understand. Self-service BI tools are putting data analysis directly into the hands of business users, without needing IT help. With more data comes greater responsibility. Data quality, security, privacy, and ethical analysis are becoming crucial. Generative AI is making advanced analytics more accessible, it is simplifying insight generation, allowing more people to use it.

Business Intelligence Issues and Challenges

4

UNIT

RATIONALE

Business Intelligence (BI) Issues and Challenges is crucial as it explores the complexities and obstacles organizations face when implementing and utilizing BI systems. It highlights challenges such as data quality, integration, privacy concerns, and the need for skilled personnel. Understanding these issues helps businesses mitigate risks, make informed decisions, and enhance their BI strategies. The unit emphasizes the importance of overcoming these challenges to fully leverage data for competitive advantage, making it highly relevant in today's data-driven business environment.

4.1 INTRODUCTION TO BUSINESS INTELLIGENCE (BI) AND ITS CHALLENGES

Business Intelligence (BI) is not just a product or system; it represents a dynamic and evolving approach that supports an organization's operations and strategic objectives. BI provides valuable insights through data analysis, enabling businesses to make informed decisions and align their operations with broader business goals. However, implementing BI comes with various challenges, and organizations often encounter significant obstacles when adopting BI systems. These challenges can hinder the successful integration of BI tools and impact the organization's ability to derive actionable insights from data. Addressing these challenges early on is critical to the success of BI initiatives.

A key component of BI includes tools like dashboards and OLAP (Online Analytical Processing). Dashboards are essential for presenting complex data in an easy-to-understand, visual format, helping decision-makers quickly interpret key performance indicators. On the other hand, OLAP systems enable multidimensional analysis of business data, helping organizations uncover trends and patterns that inform strategic decisions. Both dashboards and OLAP are integral to unlocking the full potential of BI.

4.2 CRITICAL CHALLENGES FOR BUSINESS INTELLIGENCE SUCCESS

Although BI offers many benefits, organizations face several key challenges when trying to implement successful BI systems. These challenges span organizational, technical, and strategic areas, and addressing them is vital for ensuring BI delivers the anticipated business value. The ten primary challenges organizations must tackle include:

1. **Treating BI as a Cross-Organizational Initiative:** Often, BI projects are viewed as isolated solutions rather than as part of a broader enterprise strategy. BI requires coordination across multiple departments to integrate data from various sources and provide a comprehensive view of organizational performance. Without this

holistic approach, BI initiatives may fall short in delivering the insights needed for informed decision-making.

2. **Lack of Engaged Business Sponsors:** Successful BI projects require strong backing from business leaders who can drive the initiative and ensure alignment with organizational goals. Without engaged and empowered sponsors, BI projects may lack direction and fail to secure the resources necessary for success.
3. **Insufficient Business Representation:** BI systems must be closely aligned with the needs of the business. A lack of key business stakeholders involved in the process can result in BI solutions that don't address critical organizational challenges. Effective communication between IT and business teams is essential to ensure that BI tools meet user needs.
4. **Shortage of Skilled BI Professionals:** Developing, implementing, and maintaining BI systems require expertise in data analysis, systems integration, and BI tools. A shortage of skilled professionals or improper deployment of existing talent can lead to subpar BI implementations, preventing organizations from maximizing their data assets.
5. **Absence of a Structured BI Development Methodology:** Without a clear, iterative development process, BI projects can become disorganized. Implementing BI systems without structured methodology—such as project planning, testing, and feedback loops— can result in missed objectives and failure to meet organizational goals.
6. **Lack of BI Project Planning:** Successful BI implementation requires meticulous planning, including well-defined objectives, realistic timelines, and appropriate resource allocation. Poor planning can result in project delays, cost overruns, and unmet expectations.
7. **Business Analysis and Data Standardization Challenges:** Data across departments is often stored in inconsistent formats. Without proper business analysis and data standardization, integrating and analyzing data becomes difficult. Data inconsistencies can lead to inaccurate conclusions, which undermine decision-making.
8. **Impact of Dirty Data on Profitability:** Inaccurate or incomplete data is one of the biggest barriers to BI success. Dirty data can lead to incorrect decision-making, diminishing the value that BI systems are supposed to generate.
9. **Underuse of Metadata:** Metadata, which provides context about data, is often underutilized in BI systems. Proper use of metadata is essential for ensuring data quality, improving governance, and enhancing BI tool functionality.
10. **Overreliance on Specific Tools (Silver Bullet Syndrome):** Many organizations fall into the trap of relying too heavily on specific BI tools or techniques, thinking that one solution can solve all their BI challenges. This over-reliance often leads to disappointment when the chosen tool fails to meet the organization's complex needs.

4.3 SUCCESS FACTORS FOR BUSINESS INTELLIGENCE

Despite these challenges, BI can provide immense value to organizations that navigate these obstacles effectively. The key factors for BI success include:

- **Making Better, Faster Decisions:** With the right BI systems in place, organizations can make quicker, data-driven decisions with greater confidence, improving their ability to respond to market shifts.
- **Streamlining Operations:** BI helps identify operational inefficiencies and bottlenecks, enabling organizations to optimize their processes and reduce costs.
- **Accelerating Product Development:** By utilizing insights from BI, businesses can speed up product development cycles, ensuring that products are launched in response to market needs and customer expectations.
- **Maximizing the Value of Existing Products:** BI enables businesses to identify opportunities to improve existing products or services, helping them better meet customer needs and maximize revenue.
- **Enhancing Marketing and Customer Relationships:** BI provides deeper insights into customer behavior, allowing organizations to create more targeted marketing campaigns and build stronger, personalized relationships with customers.

4.4 THE CHALLENGES WHICH ORGANIZATIONS FACE WHILE IMPLEMENTING BUSINESS INTELLIGENCE

1. Cross-Organizational Partnership
2. Business Sponsors
3. Dedicated Business Representation
4. Availability of Skilled Team Members
5. Business Intelligence Application Development Methodology.
6. Planning BI Projects.
7. Business Analysis and Data Standardization.
8. Affect of Dirty Data on Business Profitability.
9. Importance of Meta-Data.
10. Silver Bullet Syndrome.

1. Cross-Organizational Partnership

Traditionally, business plans, including decision-support projects, focused on specific goals tied to certain products or regions. This narrow focus limited organizations' ability to assess the overall impact of these projects on their broader operations. As companies shifted towards a customer-centric approach, they began to integrate customer data with product-related information. It's essential to understand that it's not just manufacturing and product managers who drive the business, but customers and market demands. Addressing customer issues proactively, even before they are fully aware of the problem, can significantly enhance loyalty. Customers are more likely to remain loyal when they feel their problems are solved, rather than when a product is merely delivered.

Previously, integration occurred within isolated departmental or regional databases, with little cross-regional collaboration. The introduction of enterprise data warehouses marked the next step towards integrating organizational information for decision-making purposes, such as sales reporting, Key Performance Indicators (KPIs), and trend analysis.

Customer Relationship Management (CRM) followed, offering opportunities to increase sales and profitability through personalized services. Now, Business Intelligence (BI) represents the next phase in achieving a holistic, cross-organizational view of operations. BI has significant potential to deliver substantial returns but requires a unique level of collaboration.

In BI, the partnership extends beyond departmental boundaries and requires integrating knowledge across various organizational levels. This includes understanding customer behavior, market conditions, competitors, suppliers, and internal teams. For BI to be successful, an organization must foster a culture of cross-organizational collaboration where every team works together toward a shared vision.

2. Business Sponsors

Strong business sponsors actually believe in the importance of the BI project. They campaign for it by removing political roadblocks. Without a helpful and dedicated business sponsor, a BI project will struggle for support within the organization and will usually fail. Business sponsors set up proper objectives for the BI application, making sure that they support the strategic idea. The sponsors also support the business case assessment which helps in setting up the project scope. If the scope is too big, the sponsors can priorities the deliverables. For most BI projects, the business sponsors also begin a data-quality campaign in the affected departments. This is a task for the business sponsors because it is the business users who have to identify the data. Finally, the business sponsors run a project review session at particular Business Intelligence checkpoints to ensure that the BI application functionality maps properly to the strategic business aims, and also on the Return on Investment2 (ROI) which can be objectively measured.

3. Dedicated Business Representation

In many Business Intelligence (BI) projects, the focus tends to be more technical than business-oriented. This is often because these projects are typically managed by IT project managers who may lack sufficient business knowledge. As a result, these managers may not engage fully with the business side of the organization, which can lead to BI projects failing to deliver the expected business outcomes. It's important to note that while BI tools are critical, only about 20% of businesspeople use them regularly, highlighting the need for strong business representation. For a BI project to succeed, it is crucial to involve business stakeholders from the beginning. These representatives should come from several key areas:

- **Business Executives:** These individuals are responsible for guiding the overall strategic direction of the organization. Their role in a BI project is to make major decisions and ensure that the project aligns with the organization's goals. They should be involved throughout the process to help steer the project and make critical decisions at various stages.
- **Finance Department:** The finance team is key to understanding the financial implications of the BI project. They can provide valuable insights into the company's efficiencies, potential cost savings, and areas for growth, helping to align BI outputs with financial goals.
- **Marketing Personnel:** Marketing teams are primary users of BI tools, and their involvement in the project is essential from start to finish. They can help define the goals of the BI system and ensure that the project delivers insights that are actionable for marketing strategies.

- **Sales and Customer Support Representatives:** These teams interact directly with customers and are integral in ensuring that the BI system reflects customer needs. By including their perspectives, the project can be designed to better meet customer expectations and improve service delivery.
- **IT Personnel:** While IT staff provide the technical support for the BI project, their role goes beyond just maintaining systems. They should also work closely with other teams to understand their requirements and help translate those needs into BI solutions.
- **Operations Managers and Staff:** Operations managers bridge the gap between strategic goals and day-to-day activities. Their involvement ensures that the BI system aligns with both the long-term strategy and the operational data, ensuring that BI insights can be used to make informed operational decisions.

4. Availability of Skilled Team Members

BI projects can vary greatly from one another due to the absence of clear, well-defined deliverables at the outset. Additionally, the business and technical skills required for BI applications differ from those needed for operational systems like Online Transaction Processing (OLTP). While operational projects tend to focus on specific areas of business, such as Enterprise Resource Planning (ERP), Customer Relationship Management (CRM), or supply chain management (SCM), BI projects involve gathering, analyzing, and integrating data from across the entire business.

The technical requirements for BI are also unique. For example, a database administrator working with OLTP systems typically focuses on optimizing data retrieval. In contrast, a BI system requires expertise not only in retrieving data but also in its effective storage and management.

A BI project team that lacks experience in BI application implementation is likely to struggle in delivering the expected results, particularly in the early stages. Given the tight deadlines and short delivery cycles often associated with BI projects, relying on an inexperienced or under-skilled team is a significant risk and should be avoided.

Key skills necessary for BI projects include

- **BI Business Analysts:** These professionals conduct cause-and-effect analysis and create business process models to assess decision-making options. They must be proficient in performing what-if analysis using established BI methodologies.
- **KPI Experts:** These individuals are experts in developing balanced scorecards. They identify Key Performance Indicators (KPIs) that meet the business's needs, calculate and report on them, and monitor performance. They must also continuously evaluate the effectiveness of KPIs and integrate them into the balanced scorecard.
- **Balanced Scorecard Experts:** These professionals design and refine scorecards that help measure success in a dynamic business environment. The balanced scorecard is a vital tool for translating an organization's strategy into specific objectives, targets, and performance metrics.
- **Data Warehouse Architects:** These individuals design both logical and physical data models for BI, including star schemas and OLAP systems. Ideally, they also have experience with tools like statistical analysis and data mining algorithms.

- **Cube Developers and Implementers:** These experts specialize in applying BI-specific data models, OLAP servers, and queries. They design and deploy intelligent data cubes for multi- dimensional OLAP analysis that meets the diverse needs of users.
- **Personalization Experts:** These professionals have experience in developing web-based BI applications that not only meet the reporting needs of a broad user base but also offer personalized experiences for each individual user.

5. Business Intelligence Application Development Methodology

BI projects to succeed, the team must stick to a plan which has clearly defined methodologies, objectives and milestones. Rather, their idea is to give cross-organizational applications. Therefore, the BI methodologies and deliverables vary.

The BI answers some of the basic questions such as the following:

- What will be delivered?
- What are the benefits and expected ROI?
- What is the total cost?
- When will it be delivered?
- Who will do it?

The answers jointly define the BI project as follows: The project deliverables will map aims to the strategic business targets. These deliverables should be measured in business terms. For example, to boost the sales by 20%, the sales data combined with pipeline data should be available to the sales teams within three days of the month's end. Project scope should align the deliverables with the BI application deployment phases and timelines. Unlike the traditional OLTP applications, the number of transactions the system can perform cannot be measures in the BI project scope.

Transactions basically signify an organization's processes, which in turn represent the functions. Since BI projects are data- intensive, and not function – intensive, their scope should be measured by the data they will convert to the target BI databases, and on how quickly this data can be available. Focus on the data is required because almost 80% of the effort in a typical BI project is spent on data-related activities. ROI for a BI project should be derived from the project deliverables. The project sponsors should measure the usefulness of the delivered BI applications after the completion of each phase to decide if the project is delivering the promised ROI. If it is not, then improvements should be made.

6. Planning BI Projects

Business Intelligence (BI) projects involve converting raw data into valuable information, which is then used to drive business actions. As such, planning a BI project is not a one-time task but an ongoing, iterative process. Throughout the course of the project, resources, timelines, scope, deliverables, and strategies need to be constantly reassessed and adjusted. The planning process for BI projects follows a cyclical approach consisting of four stages: **Plan**, **Execute**, **Monitor**, and **Enhance**.

The initial step is to review the high-level data, functionality, and infrastructure requirements for the project. This phase focuses on refining the initial requirements by adding more details and removing any ambiguities, ensuring that there is clarity about what is to be delivered.

Before finalizing the project plan, it is important to examine the operational data stores to identify any potential issues or gaps. This assessment helps ensure that the data required for analysis is in a usable state and that there are no obstacles that might arise during the data analysis phase of the project. At this stage, a detailed cost analysis is performed to determine the expenses involved in purchasing and maintaining the necessary hardware, software, network equipment, and other resources. The cost analysis also includes estimates for business analysts, IT staff, implementation services, training, and consultants. Having accurate cost estimates is essential for budgeting and managing financial resources throughout the project.

A thorough risk assessment must be conducted to identify and rank potential risks associated with the BI project. The risks are assessed based on their likelihood of occurring and their potential impact on the project. This helps the team prioritize risks and plan mitigation strategies accordingly, reducing the chances of unexpected issues derailing the project. In this phase, the organization identifies the factors that are crucial for the success of the project. These factors could include having strong support from business sponsors, realistic project timelines, and the availability of the necessary resources (such as skilled team members). Ensuring that these conditions are met increases the likelihood of the project achieving its objectives. A Project Charter is created, which serves as a formal agreement or Memorandum of Understanding (MoU) that outlines the scope, objectives, and expectations of the BI project. This document is essential for setting the direction of the project and must be approved by the business sponsors and key business representatives before moving forward.

The project plan includes a breakdown of all the tasks, resources, and timelines required to complete the project. It also outlines the dependencies between tasks and resources, ensuring that the project is structured in a way that allows for efficient execution. This plan should be mapped onto a calendar to help track progress and manage deadlines. Once the project plan is complete, the project officially begins with a kick-off meeting. During this session, all team members, business representatives, and BI sponsors come together to align on the project's objectives, roles, and responsibilities. This meeting serves as an orientation to ensure everyone involved understands the goals and expectations of the BI project.

7. Business Analysis and Data Standardization in BI Projects

BI projects are heavily reliant on data, making the management of both incoming and outgoing data essential. A crucial aspect of BI projects is thoroughly evaluating the source data. Often, business analysis challenges arise because the source data is dispersed across various data stores and formatted differently throughout the organization.

The following are key challenges encountered in business analysis and data standardization for BI projects:

(a) Identifying Business Information Needs

Business analysts often struggle to pinpoint the exact business issues the BI project needs to address. It's essential to understand how solving these issues can lead to answers for critical business questions, such as, "Why has sales revenue dropped in the fourth quarter on the West Coast?" Once these questions are clearly identified, business analysts can determine the data needed to address them. These data requirements help guide the identification of relevant sources, which are essential for the success of the BI project.

(b) Data Merging and Standardization

A significant challenge in BI projects is comprehending the amount of work involved in gathering and preparing data for analysis. Often, the data is fragmented across multiple internal systems and needs to be consolidated into a single data warehouse. This process is complex and requires considerable effort. Additionally, data requirements often extend beyond internal sources to include private and external data. As a result, data merging and standardization activities should be initiated early in the BI project to ensure that all data is properly formatted and integrated, making it ready for analysis and decision-making.

8. The Impact of Dirty Data on Business Profitability

Inaccurate or inconsistent data can cost businesses millions of dollars. It's essential to identify which data is critical to the business and understand how to clean it effectively. Dirty data— data that is inaccurate, outdated, or inconsistent—must be recognized and addressed through a structured data cleansing plan. The success of any Business Intelligence (BI) project should be linked to the financial impact of poor data quality, such as lost revenue and reduced profit margins. These financial losses stem from business problems caused by inaccurate reports, which are often the result of relying on faulty data. Despite this, many BI projects fail to quantify the financial impact of dirty data in clear, monetary terms, such as "losing ten crore rupees in quarterly revenue due to the company's failure to up-sell."

Even the best BI systems can become useless if they rely on bad data. This makes it crucial for BI projects to involve experienced business analysts who not only understand the meaning and context of the source data but also ensure its accuracy and consistency. Ignoring or underestimating the importance of data cleansing is one of the primary reasons for BI project failures.

Often, BI project managers, particularly those without sufficient experience, base their project estimates on the number of technical data conversions needed, neglecting the extensive effort required to enforce business data integrity and domain rules. For large organizations with legacy systems and outdated file structures, data cleansing efforts can represent a significant portion of the project workload. In some cases, as much as 85% of the effort can be spent on cleaning and transforming data, with only 15% spent on implementing technical data conversion rules.

Therefore, even if initial project estimates seem realistic, the need for data cleansing should be factored into the planning. It's also important to ensure that the right business representatives are fully involved in the data cleansing process to guarantee its success.

9. Importance of Metadata

Clean data alone is not enough for knowledge workers unless they can understand its context. Even valid business data becomes meaningless if its significance is not clear. Therefore, it is crucial for BI applications to not only generate clean data but also to define and manage the meaning of each data element. This context is captured in what is known as *metadata*.

Managing metadata is a vital task in BI projects because it provides a detailed description of business activities and the objects involved in those activities. Metadata helps transform raw business data into meaningful information that is essential for effective decision-making in any BI environment.

For example

- What does "profit" mean in the context of the business?
- Does every business person interpret profit the same way?
- Is there only one way to calculate profit, or are there multiple valid methods?
- If there are different interpretations of profit, should each version be represented separately?

In such cases, multiple data elements should be created, each with its unique name, definition, content rules, and relationships. All of this contextual information is part of the metadata.

Metadata plays a critical role in helping business executives navigate BI databases and assists IT personnel in managing the BI applications.

Types of Metadata

1. **Technical Metadata**: This type provides information about the structure of the BI applications and databases. It helps IT staff in managing the technical aspects of these systems, including their architecture and functionality.
2. **Business Metadata**: This type provides business users with details about the data stored in the BI applications and databases. It ensures that business users can understand the data in the context of the organization's operations.

10. Silver Bullet Syndrome

The Silver Bullet Syndrome refers to the mistaken belief that a single tool, technology, or methodology can solve all the problems of a project or significantly boost productivity. This type of thinking can be particularly detrimental in Business Intelligence (BI) projects, as it oversimplifies the complexities involved in building a successful BI system.

In practice, there is no universal solution in BI. Relying on a "one-size-fits-all" approach often leads to disappointment and setbacks. The expectation that a single tool or method can resolve every issue is rarely realistic, and the results often fall short of expectations, wasting time, resources, and effort.

4.5 THE COMPLEXITY OF A BI ENVIRONMENT

A BI environment is intricate and typically comprises various distinct components, each serving a specific purpose. These include:

1. **ETL Tools (Extract, Transform, Load)**: These tools are responsible for extracting data from various source systems, transforming it into a consistent format, and loading it into the BI data warehouse.
2. **Data Warehouse**: This is the central repository that holds both historical and current business data, forming the foundation for reporting and analytics.
3. **OLAP Servers**: These servers provide the analytical capabilities needed for quick and efficient data processing and analysis.
4. **Front-End BI Applications**: These are the tools that allow business users to interact with the data, providing features like querying, reporting, and analytics to aid decision-making.

4.6 CHALLENGES IN BI TOOL SELECTION AND IMPLEMENTATION

In many organizations, the various BI components are rolled out over several phases by different teams. Each team selects tools based on its functional needs, which leads to a diverse range of tools being used across the BI system. While this may appear to be a practical solution, it can create several challenges:

- **Increased Complexity**: The more tools integrated into the system, the more complex the environment becomes to manage. Compatibility issues between different tools can complicate integration efforts.
- **Interoperability Problems**: Tools from different vendors or built on different technology platforms may not work seamlessly together, necessitating additional work to ensure proper communication and functionality.
- **Higher Maintenance Demands**: A larger number of tools generally means more resources are needed for their administration, monitoring, and troubleshooting, leading to higher overhead costs.

The Need for Simplification

Instead of relying on a wide array of tools, BI project teams should aim to streamline the environment as much as possible. By carefully selecting a minimal set of tools that align with the overall BI strategy, teams can make the project easier to manage. This simplified approach reduces complexity, minimizes integration challenges, and decreases the administrative burden, leading to a more efficient and effective BI implementation.

Customer Pain Points

Many organizations face significant challenges, or "pain points," that necessitate the adoption of Business Intelligence (BI) solutions. These pain points highlight customer problems and needs that the business aims to address. Some of the most common customer pain points are as follows:

Sufficient Data, but Lack of Insight

Organizations may collect vast amounts of data through their operational systems, but often struggle to derive meaningful insights from that data. This lack of insight into key areas such as market trends, customer behavior, and product performance hinders the organization's ability to make informed decisions and run the business more effectively.

- **Absence of a Holistic View**: Organizations may have data spread across various departments, such as finance, sales, and manufacturing. However, they often lack a unified, consistent view of this data, which makes it difficult to assess the overall businessperformance and gain a comprehensive understanding of operations.
- **After-the-Fact Insight**: Many decision-makers only receive data after it's too late to act on it. This reactive approach makes it difficult for the organization to capitalize on emerging opportunities or address risks before they become critical.
- **Manual Data Handling**: Without a strong BI foundation, employees often resort to exporting data into spreadsheets or desktop databases. From there, they manually format, analyze, and compile reports, often repeating this tedious process every time management requires an update.

4.7 OTHER COMMON BI PAIN POINTS

- **Integration and Interoperability Issues**: Problems arise when BI tools need to integrate with other systems, such as Customer Relationship Management (CRM) and Enterprise Resource Planning (ERP) systems, which may not be fully compatible.
- **Poor Data Quality**: Low-quality data can significantly reduce the effectiveness of BI initiatives, leading to inaccurate insights and unreliable decision-making.
- **Heavy Reliance on Spreadsheets**: Despite the availability of advanced BI tools, spreadsheets remain the most commonly used tool for reporting and analysis, which can be inefficient and prone to errors.
- **Misunderstanding or Ignoring BI Data**: Many users do not know how to analyze the data produced by BI tools, leading to misinterpretation or disregard of valuable insights.
- **Too Many Reporting and Analysis Tools**: The availability of numerous reporting and analysis tools can create confusion and inefficiencies, especially when users are unsure which tool is most appropriate for their needs.

Creating a Cost-Effective, Enterprise-Friendly BI Solution

BI tools offer a wide range of functionalities, from basic reports to advanced analytical solutions tailored to specific industries and operational needs. When creating a Business Intelligence solution, companies must address two primary questions:

What Data Should Be Analyzed, and Where Will It Come From?

Many packaged applications and database vendors offer BI functionality as part of their core products. If a company plans to source all its data from these existing applications or databases, it may not need additional BI products. However, relying solely on one system could limit the analytical capabilities of the organization.

Who Will Perform the Analysis, and How Will They Obtain Results?

In the past, report and analysis requests were typically sent to the IT department, which would program the necessary code and generate the report. Today, BI tools are often used directly by executives, sales teams, and marketing professionals. As a result, businesses must understand the technical capabilities of their end users and ensure that the BI tools match their needs.

Investments and Technology Stack Considerations

To build an effective Business Intelligence solution, companies need to make new investments and upgrade existing technologies to establish a comprehensive BI technology stack. This stack will include various layers of technology, from the hardware that hosts the data at the bottom of the stack, to the portal products that deliver the data to users at the top. The goal is to create a BI infrastructure that aligns with business objectives while ensuring seamless access to data for decision-makers.

4.8 THE SEVEN-LAYER STACK IN BUSINESS INTELLIGENCE

The Business Intelligence (BI) infrastructure is often structured in a seven-layer stack that integrates various technologies to handle different aspects of BI functionality. Each layer serves a specific purpose, contributing to the overall efficiency and performance of the BI system. Here's a detailed breakdown of each layer:

1. Storage and Computation Hardware

To implement BI solutions, organizations must invest in or upgrade their data storage infrastructure. This includes systems like Storage Area Networks (SAN), Network Attached Storage (NAS), and Hierarchical Storage Management (HSM), as well as tape libraries used for archival purposes. The trend for the future is the consolidation of storage resources into a unified, enterprise-wide storage pool. This approach allows for better management, efficiency, and scalability of storage resources, which is crucial for supporting large-scale BI applications that require fast data retrieval and processing.

2. Applications and Data Sources

A successful BI solution depends on organizing and cleansing the source data. However, data often comes from a variety of systems, each using its own proprietary formats and structures. These sources can include systems like Customer Relationship Management (CRM), Supply Chain Management (SCM), and Enterprise Resource Planning (ERP), among others. The trend in the coming years is for these systems to standardize their data formats, commonly using technologies like Extensible Markup Language (XML). This standardization will help simplify integration and improve the flow of data across different systems, making it easier to use the data for BI purposes.

3. Data Integration

Data integration tools, often referred to as middleware, facilitate communication between different systems that use various communication protocols, interfaces, and data formats. Organizations need to invest in these "connectors" to integrate data from diverse source applications into the BI system. The process typically involves Extraction, Transformation, and Loading (ETL) tools, which extract data from multiple sources, transform it into a consistent format, and then load it into the data warehouse. The trend here is towards standardization through XML and web services, which enables smoother data exchanges between systems and improves overall integration efficiency.

4. Relational Databases and Data Warehouses

A critical component of a BI solution is the data warehouse, which stores and organizes large amounts of historical or tactical data. Data is often stored in relational databases, which allow for efficient querying and analysis. Organizing the data in this structured manner enables users to extract specific data elements from a larger dataset and perform detailed analyses. This layer is essential for BI, as it forms the foundation of how data is stored, retrieved, and analyzed across the organization.

5. OLAP Applications and Analytic Engines

Online Analytical Processing (OLAP) applications provide a layer of abstraction between the data storage repository and the end user's analytic tools. These applications are designed to handle complex, high-performance analytical tasks that require specialized processing power. OLAP tools enable users to perform multidimensional analyses and can provide fast query responses, making them essential for businesses that require deep insights into their data. These engines are optimized to process and analyze large volumes of data quickly, which is crucial for effective decision-making.

6. Analytic Applications

Analytic applications are the programs used to run queries against the data in order to perform both historical and predictive analyses. These applications enable users to explore data through various methods, such as "slice-and-dice" analysis, which allows for drilling down into data to uncover trends or patterns. For instance, a customer intelligence application might allow users to analyze past customer orders and payment histories, or predict how price changes could impact future sales in specific regions. These applications are key for making data-driven decisions and forecasting future trends.

7. Information Presentation and Delivery Products

Once the data has been analyzed, the results need to be presented in a way that is accessible and actionable for end users. There are several tools that provide presentation and delivery of BI results, such as dashboards that combine multiple queries and display key performance indicators (KPIs). Organizations may also use reporting tools like Crystal Reports to generate detailed reports for management. A growing trend in BI presentation is the use of XML to deliver analyses through web-based portals or mobile interfaces, such as personal digital assistants (PDAs), allowing users to access data and insights on the go.

●●●

Intentionally Left Blank!

Business Intelligence Strategy and Roadmap

5

UNIT

RATIONALE

The Business Intelligence Strategy and Roadmap unit is crucial for guiding organizations in developing and implementing effective BI systems. It helps businesses align their data management efforts with strategic goals, ensuring that data is used efficiently to improve decision-making, performance, and competitiveness. This unit emphasizes the importance of planning, data integration, scalability, and resource optimization. By creating a clear BI strategy and roadmap, organizations can foster a data-driven culture, enhance agility, and achieve long-term growth, making informed decisions based on accurate and timely insights.

5.1 WHAT IS A BUSINESS INTELLIGENCE (BI) ROADMAP?

A Business Intelligence (BI) roadmap is a strategic framework designed by BI managers and their teams to visualize and structure the entire BI process. It covers important areas such as analytics, data management, user adoption, and training. This roadmap serves as a guide to ensure all components of BI are effectively planned, executed, and maintained, enabling businesses to fully leverage their data for strategic insights.

5.2 WHY IS A BI STRATEGY IMPORTANT?

A well-defined BI strategy is essential for addressing data-related challenges, creating a unified system, and ensuring long-term maintenance. Without a clear strategy, businesses may focus too much on producing charts and reports without fully understanding their value. This can lead to inefficiency and confusion, as employees may not fully comprehend how to use the data. A BI strategy ensures that data insights are not just gathered but are applied effectively throughout the organization, helping bridge the gap between data collection and informed decision-making.

5.3 PLANNING BI IMPLEMENTATION

To implement BI successfully, companies need to conduct a detailed analysis of their specific requirements. They must select the right tools and technologies that align with their business objectives. Real-time integration tools are essential for keeping data updated, particularly those with data replication engines that ensure continuous, real-time information. Additionally, visual tools, such as analytic dashboards, are now a standard part of BI, as they help translate complex data into clear visuals that support better decision-making. BI has the potential to significantly improve a company's performance by enhancing decision-making processes. Data is often regarded as one of the most valuable assets for a company, after its workforce. By leveraging accurate and timely data, companies can make faster and more informed decisions, improving their competitive position.

Key Elements for Successful BI Implementation

1. **Real-Time Data Access:** Companies must ensure they can access real-time data quickly. Certain industries, such as banking, may require responses in milliseconds, while others can manage with updates every few minutes. The right solution should be chosen based on these time requirements.
2. **Data Integration:** Efficient integration tools are critical for handling real-time data. Although these systems can be expensive, more affordable alternatives, like native database replication or database triggers, can be used to capture and store data changes in a staging area, making it accessible for processing.
3. **Dashboards and Visual Tools:** Dashboards have become essential in BI implementations, providing an intuitive way to present complex data in an easily digestible format. These tools help users quickly derive insights from both statistical and numerical data.
4. **Choosing the Right BI Solution:** The BI system should align with how the company makes decisions. Companies must assess the types of information executives need to make confident and timely decisions and determine the most effective way to present that data.

Seven Steps for a Successful BI Deployment

1. **Ensure Data Quality:** Clean and accurate data is the foundation of any BI solution. Regular data cleaning and validation are necessary to maintain the quality of insights.
2. **Train Users Effectively:** Proper user training is critical to ensuring that employees can interact with the BI tools and interpret the data accurately. Well-trained users will make the most out of the BI system.
3. **Deploy Quickly and Adjust:** Avoid spending too much time creating the "perfect" reports upfront. Business needs evolve over time, so it is better to deploy reports that provide immediate value and then refine them based on feedback and changing requirements.
4. **Build an Integrated Data Warehouse:** When creating a data warehouse, ensure it includes all relevant data from the outset. Avoid unnecessary complexity to ensure the process runs smoothly and efficiently.
5. **Define ROI Before Implementation:** Clearly define the Return on Investment (ROI) for the BI solution from the beginning. Set specific goals and regularly monitor progress to ensure the system delivers the intended benefits.
6. **Focus on Business Objectives:** Always prioritize the company's core business goals when deploying BI. The system should be designed to align with these goals and provide actionable insights.
7. **Choose BI Software Based on Actual Needs:** Don't purchase BI software merely because it's available. Select software that meets the company's specific needs and provides insights that will directly contribute to achieving business goals.

5.4 LIMITATIONS OF BUSINESS INTELLIGENCE

While Business Intelligence (BI) systems are intended to enhance decision-making by utilizing data, they have several limitations that can hinder their effectiveness:

1. **Incomplete Data in Data Warehouses:** Data warehouses often lack the comprehensive information required to drive revenue generation. The available data may not be organized or formatted in a way that meets the specific needs of sales teams or other revenue-generating functions.
2. **Misaligned Data Relationships:** The data relationships within a warehouse may not be optimized for revenue-focused users, such as sales teams. This misalignment can lead to inefficiencies and missed opportunities for business growth.
3. **Absence of Historical Data for Trend Analysis:** Many data warehouses do not store older data, limiting the ability to track historical trends or gain long-term insights. This restricts the ability to identify patterns and forecast future performance.
4. **Data Quality Issues:** The quality of data in BI systems can be problematic. Inaccurate, inconsistent, or incomplete data can undermine the reliability of analysis, leading to questionable insights and poor decision-making.
5. **Slow Query Response Times:** BI systems may have long query response times, sometimes exceeding 10 minutes. In fast-paced environments where timely information is crucial, this delay can significantly hinder decision-making.
6. **Limited Accessibility:** Data warehouses are often complex, and typically only IT professionals or data experts have access to them. This creates barriers for business users, particularly sales teams, who may not have the technical expertise to effectively use BI tools.
7. **Underuse by Sales Teams:** Despite their potential, sales teams may not fully utilize BI tools. This may be due to the complexity of the tools or a lack of understanding of their direct relevance to sales activities, thus reducing the overall effectiveness of the BI system.
8. **Time-Consuming Query Processing:** Running queries and generating reports can be a slow and tedious process for end users. Long wait times can discourage users from fully adopting the BI system, diminishing its impact on decision-making.
9. **Separation Between Analysis and Revenue Generation:** While BI systems and data analysts provide valuable insights, they do not directly generate revenue. It is up to sales teams to take action based on these insights, making their productivity and efficiency crucial in turning data into revenue.

5.5 BUSINESS INTELLIGENCE USAGE

Companies that implement Business Intelligence (BI) systems experience numerous advantages that boost operational efficiency and overall business performance. BI significantly reduces uncertainty within organizations, enhances communication across departments, and enables rapid responses to shifts in financial conditions, customer preferences, and supply chain dynamics. By making data-driven decisions, businesses can optimize their operations, which ultimately leads to enhanced company performance.

Data is often regarded as one of the most valuable assets for any business, second only to its human resources. By utilizing accurate and timely data, companies are empowered to make well-informed decisions that foster growth. BI streamlines decision-making, allowing businesses to act quickly and accurately on insights before competitors, often resulting in a competitive edge. Additionally, BI improves customer experiences by enabling companies to respond promptly and appropriately to customer needs and concerns.

Applications of BI

Numerous businesses have recognized the immense value that BI brings to a variety of processes. Some notable applications include:

- **E-commerce Optimization:** Analyzing click-stream data helps businesses understand customer behavior and preferences, which informs better marketing strategies and improves the user experience.
- **Warranty Issue Detection:** BI tools can quickly detect warranty-related problems, allowing businesses to address product design flaws before they cause significant damage, thereby protecting their brand image and minimizing costs.
- **Fraud Detection:** BI plays a crucial role in identifying fraudulent activities and money laundering by analyzing transaction patterns and identifying unusual behaviors that may signal suspicious activity.
- **Customer Profitability and Credit Scoring:** By analyzing customer data, businesses can assess the profitability of their customers, forecast potential financial risks, and refine credit scoring models to minimize exposure to high-risk customers.
- **Product and Service Combination Insights:** BI tools help predict which product and service combinations customers are likely to buy and when, allowing companies to maximize sales opportunities by offering the right combinations at the right time.
- **Clinical Trials:** In healthcare, BI assists in analyzing data from clinical trials for experimental drugs, providing valuable insights that can help guide the development of new treatments and medicines.
- **Insurance Premium Optimization:** BI helps insurers set more accurate and competitive premium rates by analyzing various factors such as customer risk profiles, historical claims data, and market trends.
- **Predictive Maintenance:** BI tools enable businesses to predict equipment failures by analyzing maintenance records and operational data, reducing downtime and improving overall efficiency.
- **Fraud Prevention in Financial Transactions:** BI helps detect fraudulent activities in financial transactions, such as spikes in credit card or phone card usage, which may indicate stolen data or fraudulent transactions.
- **Improved Marketing Campaigns:** BI enables businesses to convert valuable business insights into actionable intelligence, improving marketing campaign performance across various channels such as direct mail, email, and social media.
- **Customer Loyalty Identification:** BI tools help businesses identify their most loyal and profitable customers while also predicting future high-value customers, allowing firms to target marketing efforts more effectively.

The Role of Customers and Competitors in BI

Customers are at the heart of any successful business, and it is vital for companies to stay in tune with their evolving preferences to remain competitive. BI helps businesses gather data on market trends, enabling them to develop innovative products and services that meet the shifting needs of their customers. Additionally, BI allows organizations to track competitor actions, providing valuable insights that help businesses refine their strategies and maintain a competitive edge in the marketplace.

Categories of Business Intelligence Usage:

The usage of BI can be divided into several categories, each addressing specific business needs:

- **Business Operations Reporting**: One of the most common forms of BI, business operations reporting involves monitoring how actual performance aligns with set goals. Reports are frequently generated on a weekly or monthly basis to evaluate progress and identify areas where improvements can be made.
- **Forecasting:** Forecasting is both an art and a science. It involves analyzing historical data to make predictions about future outcomes. While the future is inherently unpredictable, BI uses past trends, such as changes in competitor behavior or shifts in commodity prices, to inform forecasts and guide business decisions.
- **Dashboards**: Dashboards provide a visual representation of key performance indicators (KPIs) and business metrics. They offer a snapshot of business performance, allowing users to quickly assess the status of operations. Dashboards are designed to be user-friendly, providing essential information without requiring extensive analysis.
- **Multidimensional Analysis:** This type of analysis involves examining data from multiple perspectives, often referred to as "slicing and dicing." It provides deeper insights into granular data, which requires a well-structured data warehouse and experienced analysts to interpret and extract meaningful patterns.
- **Finding Correlations Among Various Factors:** A more advanced use of BI involves exploring the relationships between different business variables, such as marketing spend, customer demographics, and seasonal trends. By identifying these correlations, businesses can better anticipate future trends, optimize strategies, and make data-driven decisions that lead to improved performance.

How to Maximize the Use of Business Intelligence

In today's business environment, data plays a crucial role in shaping decisions related to customer acquisition, improving operational efficiency, and understanding competitors. Modern organizations are inundated with vast amounts of data, and the challenge lies in effectively processing and analyzing it to extract actionable insights.

As businesses increasingly rely on data, the complexity of managing and analyzing this data has grown. In the past, organizations could manage data on a smaller scale, but today, the volume, variety, and velocity of data have significantly increased. Therefore, businesses must adopt robust Business Intelligence (BI) solutions that can handle the integration, storage, and analysis of this diverse data, ultimately supporting better decision-making.

5.6 THE ROLE OF TECHNOLOGY IN BUSINESS INTELLIGENCE

Over the past few years, technological advancements have made it easier and more cost-effective to capture and store large amounts of data. Previously, BI tools were mostly used for one-time analyses. However, today's BI tools are more sophisticated and are now embedded into the ongoing processes within organizations. These tools facilitate continuous improvements in how businesses interact with their customers and operate internally.

Additionally, the cost of BI tools has decreased significantly over time, making them more accessible to businesses of all sizes. With a variety of vendors offering different levels of complexity and pricing options, companies now have a broader selection of BI tools to choose from based on their specific needs and budgets.

Leveraging BI for Competitive Advantage

The array of BI tools available today opens up a world of possibilities. For example, BI can help businesses gather data on competitors, giving them the insights needed to stay ahead in the marketplace. These tools enable organizations to forecast future trends by analyzing historical and current data. This foresight allows businesses to prepare for potential challenges and opportunities, giving them a strategic advantage in the competitive landscape.

Using Business Intelligence to Enhance Sales

One of the key areas where BI can drive significant value is in sales and marketing. By using BI to identify the most lucrative opportunities, businesses can focus their efforts on the targets that are most likely to yield a high return. Often, sales and marketing teams face roadblocks that hinder profitability. BI helps to identify these obstacles and provides the data necessary to address them effectively.

With the right intelligence, businesses can also optimize their sales processes. By using data-driven sales tools, organizations can streamline their approach, reduce inefficiencies, and ultimately increase sales. BI tools help identify patterns in sales data, revealing trends that can be leveraged to boost performance.

5.7 HOW DOES BI FUNCTION TECHNOLOGICALLY?

BI platforms comprise several layers of technology that work together to gather, analyze, and present data in meaningful ways. These technologies are built on a stack, with each layer serving a specific purpose in the overall process. Here's a breakdown of the typical BI technology stack:

- **Infrastructure:** This is the foundation of the BI system and includes the hardware and networks, such as servers, workstations, operating systems, and network connections, that support the entire BI framework.
- **Data Acquisition:** At this level, data is sourced from various organizational systems, such as payroll, accounts receivable, or customer management systems. These systems generate transactional data that serves as the basis for BI analysis.
- **Data Integration:** After data is collected, it must be integrated and cleaned. This step involves using software to extract data from multiple systems, clean it to ensure accuracy, and combine it into a unified format for analysis.

- **Data Aggregation and Storage:** Once the data is integrated, it is stored in a repository. This repository can house both raw data and summarized data, allowing for efficient querying and analysis.
- **Data Analysis:** This step involves using analytic software to query the data repository, run reports, and create "what if" scenarios. Data analysis tools provide insights into business operations and help in forecasting future trends.
- **Portal:** The portal is the interface through which managers and IT analysts access the BI tools. It provides a user-friendly environment for interacting with the data and running queries to make informed decisions.

Organizational Culture

Organizational culture refers to the collective set of beliefs, values, and norms shared within a company or organization. While often referred to as "corporate culture," this term is not entirely accurate, as even non-profit organizations or charities have their own organizational cultures. Let's explore different definitions and perspectives on organizational culture.

One common definition explains organizational culture as a collection of beliefs, values, and norms, along with symbols, key events, and influential individuals that define an organization's unique character. These elements create the context for actions within and outside the organization. The key components—beliefs, values, and norms—are central to understanding the culture. Norms can also encompass the company's traditions, authority structures, and everyday practices.

Another definition describes organizational culture as the pattern of shared assumptions developed by a group as it solves problems. These assumptions are so effective that they are considered valid and passed on to new members, shaping the way they think, act, and feel in similar situations.

A simpler interpretation of organizational culture is that it reflects the collective response of a group to external or internal stimuli. It's a group of people who have learned how to behave in specific situations, similar to social learning. In this way, corporate culture operates as a social learning process, where individuals adopt behaviors and practices based on shared experiences and the social dynamics within the organization.

Over time, organizational culture becomes deeply embedded within a company's identity, significantly influencing the individuals within it. This creates a cyclical relationship: people shape the culture, and the culture, in turn, shapes the people. As such, organizational culture serves as a guiding force, aligning employees with the company's core values and practices.

5.8 KEY CHARACTERISTICS OF ORGANIZATIONAL CULTURE

Organizational culture is influenced by various psychological, attitudinal, and experiential factors. It embodies the collective experiences, successes, failures, values, and beliefs of the organization. Because culture is so deeply ingrained, changing it is a complex process that requires substantial time, resources, and effort. When attempting to change organizational culture, companies may need to bring in external consultants who can offer fresh perspectives, as those immersed in the current culture may struggle to see things objectively. Though there are various definitions of organizational culture, they all highlight common themes: shared experiences, routines, values, beliefs, goals, and systems that are passed down and learned over time. These elements form the core identity of an organization.

5.9 VALUES AND NORMS IN ORGANIZATIONAL CULTURE

Organizational culture is closely tied to the shared values and norms among its members. Values represent the beliefs about what the organization should aim to achieve, while norms define how employees should behave to reach those objectives. The organization's values and norms not only guide behavior but also shape interactions with others, both inside and outside the company.

From these values, organizational norms are formed. These norms establish the expected behaviors for employees in different situations, ensuring alignment with the company's goals. In doing so, norms create a standard set of expectations for how individuals should act within the organization.

Organizational Culture vs. Corporate Culture

Though often used interchangeably, "corporate culture" is a subset of organizational culture. Corporate culture refers to the values, customs, traditions, and practices that set one company apart from another. It is often seen as the character of the organization, reflecting the vision of its founders. The values within corporate culture can influence the moral standards and behaviors of the company's members.

Corporate culture can be shaped by senior management, who may define the company's values and behaviors to align with the organization's objectives. However, within any organization, subcultures exist. Different workgroups may develop their own distinct behaviors and interactions that influence the overall corporate culture. Unlike organizational culture, which evolves over time, corporate culture can sometimes be imported. For instance, a computer technician may bring their expertise and professional behaviors to the company, impacting the broader corporate culture.

5.10 THE ROLE OF ORGANIZATIONAL CULTURE IN SHAPING BEHAVIOR

Organizational culture is often described as a deeply ingrained, subconscious set of rules and codes that determine the "feel" of the organization. It establishes what is considered acceptable or unacceptable, important or unimportant, and effective or ineffective. These cultural norms guide how the organization responds to crises, changes, or external challenges. New employees must learn this cultural code to know how to behave and interact within the organization.

Organizational culture reflects the company's history, experiences, values, and assumptions. It is expressed through the company's self-image, internal processes, external interactions, and future expectations. Over time, the culture develops unwritten rules and shared beliefs that have been proven to work effectively. These cultural elements help bind the organization together and shape its identity.

How Organizational Culture Impacts Business Operations

Organizational culture significantly influences how a business operates, how it treats employees, and how it engages with the broader community. Key aspects of organizational culture include:

1. **Business Conduct:** The way the company conducts its business and interacts with customers, employees, and the community.

2. **Autonomy and Freedom:** The level of freedom employees have in decision-making, expressing ideas, and contributing new concepts.
3. **Power and Data Flow:** How power is distributed and how information flows through the company hierarchy.
4. **Employee Commitment:** The level of dedication employees have toward the company's objectives.

The strength of an organization's culture is often referred to as "strong" or "weak," depending on how widely it is ingrained throughout the company. A strong culture typically drives better productivity, performance, customer service, product quality, and safety. It also influences approaches to marketing, advertising, and new product development. The unique and often deeply-rooted nature of organizational culture makes it difficult to change and is often summed up with the phrase, "It's how we do things here."

5.11 MANAGING TOTAL COST OF OWNERSHIP (TCO) IN BUSINESS INTELLIGENCE

Total Cost of Ownership (TCO) is a critical metric for understanding the costs associated with developing and operating Business Intelligence (BI) programs. TCO provides valuable insights into calculating the Return on Investment (ROI) for BI initiatives. Traditional TCO models focus primarily on visible costs like hardware, software, telecommunications, and personnel expenses related to development and support. However, these models often overlook an important component: the time and costs incurred by business analysts who use the information. To gain a more accurate understanding of the costs, companies should look beyond traditional TCO models and manage the costs associated with information delivery. This includes accounting for the time business analysts spend capturing, validating, recording, and correcting data. Without factoring in these time costs, the true financial impact of BI projects may be underestimated.

Enhancing TCO Management

When calculating TCO, it is important to include the time spent by business analysts on data management tasks. For instance, when transitioning from a data mart to an enterprise data warehouse, the time spent on data validation and correction should be part of the TCO calculation. Business analysts often devote a significant portion of their time to these tasks, leaving only a small amount of time for actual data analysis. By managing TCO effectively, companies can optimize BI programs and use resources more efficiently.

Surveys can be used to gather data on the time business analysts spend on various tasks. For example, questions could focus on how much time is spent searching for information, reconciling data from multiple sources, or correcting errors. By tracking these metrics over time, organizations can identify areas for improvement and prioritize their BI efforts.

Managing TCO for information delivery is essential for the success of a BI program. It goes beyond traditional cost considerations and emphasizes the importance of accounting for the time and effort spent turning raw data into actionable business insights.

Factors Influencing Total Cost of Ownership (TCO)

The factors that contribute to the Total Cost of Ownership (TCO) in Business Intelligence (BI) are interconnected, meaning a change in one area can significantly impact others. It is important to evaluate the entire system when making decisions, as removing or altering one component could have a ripple effect on other parts. A successful BI strategy must:

- Cater to the diverse needs of all users.
- Support the creation of custom BI applications.
- Be compatible with existing data.
- Function across different platforms.
- Require minimal ongoing support and maintenance.

As a business grows and its data demands increase, the costs associated with supporting and providing these services can rise substantially. Additionally, if BI applications are meant for public access, such as being available to customers, their performance and reliability will directly affect the organization's reputation. Therefore, it is crucial to manage these costs effectively to ensure long-term success.

5.12 HARDWARE AND SOFTWARE EXPENSES

The costs tied to hardware and software across an organization can accumulate quickly. When many users are accessing BI applications simultaneously, the expenses for purchasing additional processors, maintaining server licenses, and providing support staff become significant. Over time, these costs can become inefficient, especially when various tools and systems do not integrate well or are underutilized.

To mitigate these expenses, organizations should focus on improving their return on investment (ROI) by opting for cost-effective solutions that can scale to meet growing data needs. Web-based solutions, in particular, are beneficial because they usually don't require per-user client licenses and often don't need extra software on the client side, which helps reduce overall costs.

Software Functionality

Organizations typically have a diverse range of users, from casual users who need basic data insights to more advanced users, such as analysts or power users, who require deep data analysis and report generation. For a BI solution to be effective, it must empower all users to create reports, conduct complex queries, and perform detailed analysis using just a web browser. If the solution requires significant training or has complex tools that are difficult to master, it will not be cost-effective in the long run. To minimize TCO, the solution should feature an intuitive interface that is easy to use, with minimal learning required. It should not depend on plug-ins and should be simple enough for users to begin utilizing right away. The aim is for the entire organization to adopt the solution easily, without a steep learning curve.

Software Architecture and Scalability

When selecting a vendor for a BI solution, it is essential to consider not only the cost of the software but also the hardware specifications needed to support it. A solution that leverages the internet to transfer data to and from users at all levels tends to be the most efficient.

Simply increasing hardware capacity, such as adding processors, won't solve the core issue of supporting a growing number of users who require real-time access to accurate data. A scalable BI solution reduces the need for additional hardware and lowers maintenance costs, all while meeting the needs of an expanding user base. As users gain more independence, IT resources can be reallocated from responding to urgent business requests to focusing on broader strategic initiatives that benefit the entire organization.

In evaluating BI solutions, organizations should factor in the complete costs involved in purchasing, deploying, and operating the system. A practical approach to reducing TCO is to select the most cost-effective vendor, particularly in areas like parameterized and user-defined reporting, available on both Windows and UNIX platforms. This is especially beneficial for large-scale environments, and in certain cases, it can lead to substantial savings—potentially hundreds of thousands of rupees, depending on the number of users (e.g., 1,000 or 10,000 users). By choosing a vendor offering the best value in these categories, organizations can significantly lower the overall costs of their BI implementation.

Time to Implement

One of the main challenges in implementing Business Intelligence (BI) systems is the high cost of developer resources. Developers are essential for building BI applications, but they can be expensive. At the same time, users require quick and constant access to accurate information, which means BI applications need to be deployed rapidly across the organization. To address this, developers should be provided with flexible tools that enable the swift creation and deployment of BI applications tailored to the needs of different user groups. These tools must be capable of efficiently developing complex BI applications, ensuring they are user-friendly and optimized for productivity.

A BI solution should offer an open, intuitive environment that facilitates the fast development of web-based reports or information systems. This enables developers to quickly create applications, ensuring business users have immediate access to the information they need. Rapid deployment is critical to fulfilling business demands, and an intuitive development environment is essential to keeping both implementation time and costs to a minimum.

User Training

Ensuring that users can effectively access and analyze the information they need is a crucial part of deploying a BI solution. However, the question remains: are the users fully prepared to use the BI system? To minimize Total Cost of Ownership (TCO), organizations should aim to keep both the time and costs associated with training diverse user groups as low as possible. Users—from executives to partners, customers, and analysts—should be empowered to quickly access data, perform analysis, and create reports without needing extensive training.

The goal is to make the solution user-friendly so that employees at all levels can complete their tasks with minimal assistance. The system should allow users to easily manage and share information across the organization, ensuring that results can be saved, viewed, printed, or taken offline for further analysis. A system that is easy to use adds more value to the BI solution and increases Return on Investment (ROI). By minimizing the learning curve, organizations can extract more value from the BI system while reducing the need for intensive training and ongoing support.

Support and Maintenance

A significant portion of TCO comes from the support and maintenance required to keep a BI system operational. If IT staff are frequently addressing simple user requests, this will increase costs and put pressure on resources. To reduce these costs, the BI solution should be easy to maintain and manage. A strong BI solution will empower users to be more self-sufficient, allowing them to quickly access information, run simple queries, and even create or modify reports independently.

When users can handle basic requests themselves, IT resources can be redirected to focus on more complex issues and strategic projects. This reduces the demand for constant IT support, freeing up technical staff to concentrate on higher-value tasks. By selecting a reliable and easy-to-manage BI solution, organizations can lower TCO while ensuring that IT resources are used more effectively.

5.13 DATA ARCHITECTURE

The data architecture within an organization plays a vital role in the success of a BI solution. Often, there are significant investments in existing BI systems that should not be discarded simply due to cost concerns. Instead, organizations should focus on cleaning up the data, removing redundant or irrelevant information, and eliminating overlapping technologies that contribute to inefficiencies.

Organizations should consolidate their server resources and streamline their systems to enhance interoperability within the BI environment. The aim is to improve operations by making data easily accessible, analyzable, and manipulable, while also reducing costs associated with outdated or redundant tools. By leveraging existing BI investments and aligning them with the new solution, organizations can improve performance and productivity while minimizing operational expenses.

A fragmented BI strategy, where multiple tools are deployed and operate in isolation, often results in inefficiency and higher costs. This fragmentation can cause problems like inconsistent data views across departments or teams. Research shows that disconnected systems are costly and often introduce more complications than they resolve. Organizations should manage their current BI assets effectively and choose a solution that integrates well with their existing data and systems. This approach ensures that the BI solution is compatible with the organization's infrastructure, reducing TCO and avoiding the issues of fragmented strategies.